Meditations on Diplomacy

Comparative Cases in Diplomatic Practice and Foreign Policy

STEPHEN CHAN

E-INTERNATIONAL RELATIONS PUBLISHING

E-International Relations
www.E-IR.info
Bristol, England
2017

ISBN 978-1-910814-33-8 (paperback)
ISBN 978-1-910814-34-5 (e-book)

Production: Michael Tang
Cover Image: donskarpo via Shutterstock

A catalogue record for this book is available from the British Library

E-IR Open Access

Series Editor: Stephen McGlinchey
Copy Editor: Jane Kirkpatrick
Editorial Assistance: Naomi McMillen, Kanica Rakhra, Patricia Salas Sanchez and Farah Saleem

E-IR Open Access is a series of scholarly books presented in a format that preferences brevity and accessibility while retaining academic conventions. Each book is available in print and e-book, and is published under a Creative Commons CC BY-NC 4.0 license. As E-International Relations is committed to open access in the fullest sense, free electronic versions of all of our books, including this one, are available on the E-International Relations website.

Find out more at: http://www.e-ir.info/publications

About E-International Relations

E-International Relations is the world's leading open access website for students and scholars of international politics, reaching over three million readers per year. E-IR's daily publications feature expert articles, blogs, reviews and interviews – as well as student learning resources. The website is run by a non-profit organisation based in Bristol, England and staffed by an all-volunteer team of students and scholars.

http://www.e-ir.info

Abstract

Diplomacy is an evolving practice in terms of historical circumstance and changing national interests. History and interests do not always coincide. This book explores in brief, pungent case examples, the challenges diplomacy faces today as actors seek to change history and undermine interests.

About the Author

Stephen Chan OBE was Foundation Dean of Law and Social Sciences at SOAS University of London, where he remains as Professor of World Politics. He has occupied many named chairs around the world, most recently the Konrad Adenauer Stiftung Chair of Academic Excellence at Bir Zeit University in 2015, and the George Soros Chair of Public Policy at Central European University in 2016. He was the 2010 International Studies Association Eminent Scholar in Global Development. As an international civil servant he helped pioneer modern electoral observation in Zimbabwe in 1980, worked in many post-conflict zones – where 'post' was a largely fictional if politic appellation – and continues to be seconded to many diplomatic initiatives around the world today.

To Petros Solomon and Aster Yohannes

My friends and students of diplomacy who died unjust deaths

Contents

Introduction

I have been lecturing on diplomacy for many years, not only in academic institutions but for government ministries. This began in the early 1990s, both in the run-up to independence for Eritrea and in the first few years afterwards – when I trained its new Ministry of Foreign Affairs. This was before the country's turn to intolerance and the subsequent imprisonment and execution of its first Minister of Foreign Affairs – one of Eritrea's liberation generals and my student, Petros Solomon. It is to him, who deserved so much better, and to his wife who also died in prison, Aster Yohannes, herself a considerable liberation fighter, that I dedicate this book.

My lectures and meditations on them developed over the years after Eritrea. Their most recent iterations have been at the University of Johannesburg School of Leadership under Dr Sydney Mufamadi, Nelson Mandela's youngest minister at the moment of freedom in South Africa; and at Bir Zeit University in Palestine when I was, in 2015, the inaugural Konrad Adenauer Stiftung Chair of Academic Excellence. In 2016 I was elected the George Soros Chair in the School of Public Policy at Central European University (CEU) in Budapest. This book comprises the rewritten texts of the lectures and reflections I delivered to my graduate seminar group there. There is a series of filmed ten minute summaries of each of these lectures on https://www.youtube.com/playlist?list=PLPp1F7IFcKeBFtJz4KBo_tuTPCGwW79bT. My thanks to the CEU's Dorothy Lineer who produced these films. I want to thank my students in Asmara, Johannesburg , Ramallah, Budapest, and also at SOAS in London, for always challenging everything I said. The present book owes to their challenges. My Palestinian students at Bir Zeit will smile at this.

The reflections or meditations derive not only from my studies, but my years as an international civil servant for the Commonwealth Secretariat, and from the many diplomatic initiatives and high commands to which I have continued to be seconded in the years since. These have included work in the war zones of Africa to high-level talks in the world's great capitols. I wish to thank everyone in many places and times who helped me – or who put up with my clumsy efforts to do something for international relations.

1

Theories of Foreign Policy and International Relations

Diplomacy is not new. It has assumed various characteristics in the modern age, but the idea of sending emissaries to another state is old and was common to many cultures. In the 19th century King Lobengula of the Ndebele nation, in what is now Zimbabwe, dispatched ambassadors to Queen Victoria to protest encroachment on his territories by British settlers and adventurers. An earlier Queen, Elizabeth I, received the Moroccan ambassador at her court, and his portrait still hangs in the Tate Britain gallery. In the wake of Henry VIII's rejection of Catholicism, Elizabeth deliberately sought diplomatic allies in the North African states – Islamic states – in the struggle against Catholic Spain. In fact, the image of North African statesmen and military men was not uncommon in Elizabethan England, and gave rise to Shakespeare's *Othello*, a play featuring a 'Moorish' admiral in the service of the Venetian navy. Not only was Othello accorded noble attributes, he married a white European wife – and the inter-racialism provoked no public outrage. The cosmopolitan nature of Elizabethan diplomacy and art was a feature of a hugely creative, if also bloody, era.

We shall see echoes of the Elizabethan outreach to North Africa later, in the case of the very young USA and its search for diplomatic recognition in the face of British antagonism and a European command of the international relations of the day. However, we begin with an observation that, while diplomacy is old, its service on behalf of a particular kind of state reaches back to only early modern times. In fact, diplomacy as we know it, is a foundation attribute of the advent of modernity.

This particular kind of state was what arose from the lengthy deliberations that led to the Peace of Westphalia in 1648. This was at the end of the 30 Years War that devastated Europe. The entire continent was militarised, even if some countries avoided the worst of the conflict. The internal feuds and armed suspicions by rival groups, as epitomised by Alexander Dumas's *The Three Musketeers*, reflected the mood within Europe at large. In the Middle European region, however, the conflict was savage and the devastation extensive. The continent then was an assemblage of often tiny states. 194 of them were represented by 179 ambassadors at Westphalia – and much of the early deliberations were about the seating plan. Since, however, the wars had been religious, one of the key principles of the treaties that emerged was to do with the secularity of the state system. Another was that diplomacy was possible by congress, i.e. multilateral diplomacy in this case worked to end an era of turbulence. Most important was the sense that a member state of the international system should have a recognised sovereignty; recognition meant that there was a limit to how far states could intervene against the borders of another.

Of course, these principles were more honoured in the breach than actual practice in the years that followed. Napoleon clearly wreaked havoc against the borders of neighbouring states. But he also brought with his conquests an era of constitutionalism, in which citizens had rights against their rulers. Despite his defeat, the idea of rights within states remained. The question was the extent to which rights could become a trans-state, an international, norm. Beethoven's 9th Symphony, using Schiller's lyrics, celebrated the aspiration to a universal brotherhood. Before that question could be addressed, the Congress of Vienna, 1814-18, was convened to ensure there could never be another Napoleon, and established the sense of a concert of power. There might be a congress of states, but the most powerful states would score the music and conduct its performance. Rogue performers could not be in the orchestra. Beautiful lyrics were fine, provided the conductor controlled the way they were sung.

The idea of a concert was repeated after World War II, with the establishment of the United Nations – a congress for multilateral diplomacy – but it had a Security Council, a concert master. To Henry Kissinger, it seemed an ideal form of international relations. His Harvard PhD was about the outcome of the Congress of Vienna, and he applied the idea of a concert, and concert master, to all his practice of diplomacy as US National Security adviser and Secretary of State.

The state and power

The sense of powerful states, with not only their sovereign interests, but their interests in projecting a control over the international relations of the state system, became the foundation concept of a new academic discipline established after World War I. The carnage of that conflict, this time accomplished with a technology unheard of in the 30 Years War, prompted the US President to leave his country for a full six months to impose his sense of how the international system should be orchestrated. The Woodrow Wilson principles seemed to many so inspiring that the first Chair of what came to be called International Relations was endowed and established by Welsh millionaire and philanthropist, David Davies, at the University of Wales Aberystwyth, and called the Woodrow Wilson Chair.

Essentially, those principles were concerned with diplomatic transparency and international cooperation. The League of Nations was established as a multilateral assembly for diplomatic cooperation. Wilson's effort in Europe – he was the first serving US President to visit Europe, and the first to meet the Pope – greatly dissipated his health. His long absence also meant his leverage over his own Senate had waned. The treaty that emerged from the European discussions was not ratified by the Senate; the US never joined the League of Nations, and this meant there was no concert master at the heart of a congress of states that proved ineffectual. Japan invaded China, Italy invaded Abyssinia (now Ethiopia) and, despite impassioned appeals to the League from the invaded countries, the League could do nothing to protect its own members from the projection of power by other members.

While this was going on, the debates on International Relations as a new academic discipline established two principal schools of thought. One was certainly what we now call Realism, with its centrality of the state and the projection of state power on behalf of state interests; the other was an Idealism or Utopianism that suggested a broader foundation for international cooperation in citizen organisations and multilateral diplomacy. The high moral tone that seemed to have emanated from Wilson was part of this Idealism, establishing the beginnings of a normative concern for International Relations – but Wilson had also boasted that it was the US, with its values and norms, that had shown it was leading the world. "At last the world knows America as the saviour of the world."[1] The high morality was a US morality, even if based on the European thought that had inspired the American Revolution, and they were the moral norms of the most powerful state in the world.

Realist power has never, in any case, existed by itself, but always with a normative shadow shrouded in international law. It has always meant an International Relations as a discipline, as well as international politics as practice and policy, being divided, somewhat schizophrenic, but with one side of its concerns being unable to achieve freedom from the other. The entire

---

[1]   An address in Portland Oregon, 15 September 1919. www.presidency.ucsb.edu/ws/?pid=117383

assemblage also has to confront the decidedly atheoretical, and simply messy, phenomenon of foreign policy formulation. The nuts and bolts nature of this, its arguments and even pettiness – even in times of crisis – have meant no normative conceptualisation of foreign policy formulation. Studying it is an applied 'science', and diplomacy is an applied practice emanating from states and their policies, with outcomes messily achieved. If anything, it is 'organisational theory', as taught in business schools, that can be usefully deployed in the study of foreign policy formulation. One particular crisis, studied in some depth by Graham Allison, illustrates these points. As described below, Allison proposed three models of policy formulation. Each is discussed in turn in the next section.

Essence of decision

The 1962 Cuban missile crisis was a moment of grave jeopardy for the world, as nuclear confrontation between the US and the Soviet Union seemed inevitable. Following upon a failed, CIA-supported invasion of Cuba by exiles the year before, the Chairman of the Soviet Council of Ministers and Party Secretary, Nikita Khrushchev, seemed determined both to strengthen his Cuban ally and to test the mettle of the young US President Kennedy. His policy was to arm Cuba with missiles capable of bearing nuclear warheads – pointed at the US. This alarmed the US as a genuine security threat and the warning went out to the Soviet Union that its ships, carrying such weapons to Cuba, would be stopped on the high seas by US naval vessels. In international law this would have been illegal. Without a declaration of war, ships had freedom on the high seas. Also, a state, under the Westphalian doctrine, could acquire arms and another state could send them. But the determination to counter threats, particularly those launched or aided and abetted by European powers, had been a US concern since the Monroe doctrine of 1823 – which basically determined Latin America as a US sphere of influence, and a zone of exclusion for the great European powers. In 1962, the Soviet ships refused to turn back and sailed ever closer to Cuba and the US naval blockade.

The question the watching world was asking was a simple one: who would blink first? Would the tough Soviet Chairman try to sail his ships through the blockade and, if so, would the US warships sink them? If it came to that, nuclear war seemed imminent. In the end, it was the Soviet ships that turned around. It was seen as a great triumph of brinksmanship for the young President. In the account of Robert Kennedy, then Attorney-General and a member of his older brother's 'war cabinet', it was down to the steely determination of the President and his closest advisers who, even when moments of great uncertainty set in, did not waver and adhered to a path of great risk but calculated rationality.[2] Would the Soviets risk huge destruction in Russia for the sake of arming Cuba? Any war would destroy Cuba as well. Graham Allison, in his 1971 study, *Essence of Decision*, argued however that there was probably no single straight line rationality that was decisive.[3] Allison proposed three models of foreign policy formulation – and his models are still used as analytic tools to this day.

The 'Rational Actor' model is one which the US public probably ascribed to President Kennedy. In fact, as Allison said, a lot of facts have to be ignored to make scenarios fit within a 'rational' framework. Acting rationally, the US anticipated that, if the Soviets also behaved rationally, they would turn back. Mutually Assured Destruction (MAD, as the nuclear jargon of those days had it) was too high a price to pay for Cuba.

The 'Organisational Process' model is a persuasive one in that, in any moment of crisis, a government will seek to break down the crisis into component parts and assign each part to a specialist governmental agency or department. The Department of Defense would know more about military matters than the State Department, but the State Department would know more about diplomatic options. However, in a moment of crisis, when time is short, pre-existing plans and options that reflect the ethos and inclinations of the department concerned, in short 'repertoire' plans and responses, would likely be used. This means that, even in a highly organised government, crisis diplomacy may not be exactly fitted to the nature of the crisis at hand. Often, the first proposed form of response that 'fits' may be used for want of another that might fit better but take more time to devise. In the case of the Cuban missile crisis, Kennedy contemplated a surgical airstrike against the Soviet equipment that had already reached Cuba – but the only pre-existing airforce plans were based on saturation bombing that would also cause huge collateral damage. A naval blockade became the best pre-existing plan of action.

Under the 'Governmental Politics' model, those department chiefs under the President may argue; if they do not argue, they may be 'yes men', appointed by the President precisely because they are 'yes men' and the quality of their advice may suffer; but, in moments of extreme crisis, even a confident and very powerful President would have to negotiate or utilise political techniques to get his way, at the very least to avoid having his orders misunderstood or actioned in a way he had not intended. In a democracy, he must use political

---

[2]   Robert F. Kennedy, *Thirteen Days: A Memoir of the Cuban Missile Crisis*, New York: Norton, 1969.

[3]   Graham T. Allison, *Essence of Decision: Explaining the Cuban Missile Crisis*, New York: Little Brown, 1971.

techniques to convince the legislature and the public he is correct. The failure of the 1961 invasion of Cuba by dissident exiles – the Bay of Pigs fiasco – had led Kennedy to distrust the advice of the CIA. In order to keep his military advisers on side, both Kennedy brothers attacked the diplomatic avenues proposed by UN Ambassador, Adlai Stevenson. Within the military, Kennedy had to manoeuvre opinion away from air strikes towards the blockade. The naval blockade thus emerged from a political process, but Kennedy also had to make certain political gestures so that the Soviet leader could save his own political face. Kennedy agreed never to invade Cuba. He instructed his brother, Robert Kennedy, to promise the Soviets privately that US missiles in Turkey – missiles that could reach the Soviet Union easily – would be withdrawn a few months later.

The essence of decision probably involved aspects of all three models. Whatever the ratio in the mix, the decision to launch a naval blockade – even though with fewer risks than an aerial onslaught – was one with huge difficulties and unavoidable risks that could not be removed. The size and calibre of those risks were such that no decision-making process could be assured of success, and certainly not safety or even survival. Allison's three models are illuminating when applied to the US situation, especially with this particular case example. However, there are dangers in a universal application, despite apparent similarities in different conditions in different countries.

A brief meditation

Even in the case used by Allison, the Cuban missile crisis, such analysis of the Soviet situation as his book contained was purely speculative. We do not know the manner of Khrushchev's policy-making apparatus, nor the weight he was able to give to any part of it; nor do we know how he weighed the US policies and ultimatums – how he, in rational calculations, weighed what was bluff and what had substance. We do not know what kind of specialist advisers he used, what branches of the government and military they represented and, above all, what role the Communist Party and the Politburo played. The idea of not only a government, but a commissariat over the government, each with its bureaucratic and organisational processes, and politics, makes the Soviet situation even more difficult to analyse than the US one.

We do not have an elegant testimony by Khrushchev's younger brother, like Robert Kennedy's, solemnly setting out a version of how a group of what seemed to be intrinsically decent men pondered the fate of the world.

What the American pundits called 'Kremlinology', analysing Moscow's foreign policy intentions, became a game involving guess-work as much as arcane forms of knowledge.

In the case of early-Cold War China, especially after the McCarthy witch-hunts had forced John Service and the majority of Sinologists and Chinese-speakers out of the State Department, there was no way that the US could reliably decipher Beijing's foreign policy. There, the separable but inter-connected forms of apparatus of government, party, and military to this day make Beijing-watching a hazardous process – and is made considerably more hazardous by the addition of China's vast fiscal and economic machinery as it lays out a new world order of Chinese domination.

In recent times, reading Tehran, with its vexed power-plays and intensely complex checks and balances in the constitutional and theological maze that represents the politics of Iran, even being an expert on Shi'a Islam would give an analyst only one part of the picture of how Tehran sought to approach negotiations on nuclear capacity; that, allied to the immense skills of its diplomats – who, to all intents and purposes, represented an enigma – made negotiations with the regime something far from amenable to secular rationality and calculation.

Finally, in the case of the African state of Zambia, when its President Kenneth Kaunda – against the advice of other African Presidents – entered negotiations in 1989 with the new South African President F.W. de Klerk, he did so without any regard for the foreign policy apparatus behind him. There were no organisational processes or governmental politics. He just did it all himself. But he had no grounds for rational action. He had not a single briefing note on de Klerk (de Klerk had five volumes of notes on Kaunda). Kaunda did it by intuition and a huge trust in the moral force he convinced himself could move the mountain of the Apartheid state. A crucial moment in Zambian foreign policy, which all the same was instrumental in hastening the end of Apartheid, cannot ever be analysed or deciphered by any, or any combination of Allison's models.

Discursive formations and foreign policy

As International Relations theory has developed since 1918, competitive but overlapping schools of thought have arisen. Always, however, the state has remained in place as a central actor, with debate over the extent to which it is the only actor. Schools that concentrate on pluralism have emphasised international organisation and citizen groups. Structuralist schools have argued that the state is the articulation of other forces such as capital and class. More recently, the so-called English School has invested Realism with a renewed historical foundation. A state's history provides a context for analysing its decisions.[4] The Copenhagen School has added discursive formations to the historical context. How the state constructs discourse, and is in turn constructed by prevailing discourse, has huge impact on the formulation of foreign policy.[5] The implication of the Copenhagen School is that there must be a government machinery that undertakes discursive formation and reinforcement that is far beyond the apparatus of foreign policy and diplomacy – and links foreign policy much more closely to the central concerns of the state than before, i.e. it is not separable from the demands of domestic policy. We shall, later in this book, look at Uriel Abulof's account of discursive forces in Israel, and how they have led to an immense 'securitisation' of the state, its forces, and its foreign policy.

A coda as meditation: The Middle East as a falsifier or antagonist of the Westphalian state

As we write, the focus of the world's diplomacy is on two areas. Russian President Putin's annexation of Crimea, and his perceived 'new' expansionism of foreign policy – on behalf of a state that is still massively nuclear-armed - will be discussed a little later. The other area is the Middle East, with the turmoil caused by the Islamic State of Iraq and Syria (ISIS); and with the dawning realisation that some of the state actors in the region may be playing, or at least tolerating its senior personnel and institutions playing a double game. In his latest (and probably last) book, Henry Kissinger airs his suspicions of Saudi Arabia being an ostensible member of the Westphalian system, but for confessional reasons supporting the propagation of what is proposing itself as an Islamic state system.[6] This too will be discussed towards the end of this book. It is a real challenge to the foundations of International Relations theory, as well as a major complication in foreign policy formulation and diplomacy. It is a challenge to theory since Westphalia sought to secularise the international system, and there are few well-developed tools for conceptualising a resacralised world, especially one resacralised not even in its previous Christian sense, but an Islamic one. The last time the world had a Christian/Western and Islamic clash was hundreds of years ago. It is a challenge to policy and practice since confessional values do not fit well into any of the models someone like Allison put forward. If Kennedy and his advisers calculated there would be a moment of rational

---

[4]   Barry Buzan, *An Introduction to the English School of International Relations: The Societal Approach*, Cambridge: Polity, 2014.

[5]   Barry Buzan, Ole Waever, Jaap de Wilde, *Security: A New Framework for Analysis*, Boulder: Lynne Rienner, 1998.

[6]   Henry Kissinger, *World Order: Reflections on the Character of Nations and the Course of History*, London: Allen Lane, 2014, espec. Pp 134-141.

lucidity in which the Soviets, projecting the costs, would back down – there is no guarantee that worldly costs would trump the anticipated values of Godly blessing.

It may be that what we see today is fleeting, or that the challenge against Westphalia turns out to be the attempt at falsification that, finally, renders the Westphalian system 'true' and durable. Or it could be a genuine antagonism that is determined to supplant the Westphalian system, or at least marginalise it in favour of a new world order. It could even be that there is a discrepancy of aim between Saudi and ISIS strategists – with the former certainly testing the durability of today's system but ultimately content should their efforts prove only to be an act of unsuccessful falsification, and Saudi Arabia continues to benefit from its place in the international system; for them, it might be a kind of win-win situation; and the latter hell-bent on overthrow, knowing military force is not good at destroying an idea, and knowing that today's diplomatic practice is not shaped for religious conflict.

2

Feet of Iron and Clay: US and British Foreign Policy and Diplomacy from One Regime Change to Another

It is a favourite prophetic image for many Christian sects with an apocalyptic vision – in which the international systems of man are finally destroyed by the rock of Heaven, which then fills the earth with its magnificence and durable holiness. There is almost an exact parallel between this vision and that of ISIS – the Christian version being articulated most visually in the book of Daniel (2:31-35). There, the Babylonian king dreams of a great statue, made from various metals, the head being made of the most valuable metal and the torso becoming progressively less valuable until, finally, the feet are an uneasy amalgam of iron and clay. It is these feet with their clay fault-lines that the rock of Heaven strikes, and the entire history of human empires and world orders collapses into dust. The prophet Daniel interprets the dream for the king, but his interpretation is taken further forwards by the apocalyptic sects of today. Not all are agreed as to the identity of the feet, but one view suggests that the golden head is the Babylonian world order; the silver chest represents the Persian world order; the bronze loins the Greek world order; the iron legs the Roman; and the weak mixture that makes up the feet the Anglo-American world order. It is a peculiarly Judeo-Christian and Western-centric historical line – with no mention of a Mongol world order, an Islamic world order, a Chinese empire, a Russian empire or an Ottoman empire. And there is a long gap between the fall of Rome and the advent of the British empire and Britain's different forms of relationship with the US – beginning as colonial master and ending in the present day as dependent courtier. Even so, the image of an uneasy alliance – iron and clay – an unsteady one, reflects a contemporary reality. And it is not just ISIS that imagines it could be the rock of Heaven; China and a resurgent Russia may have occasional inclinations to be such a rock. The European Union (EU) probably already feels that it, and not Britain, constitutes the clay seeking to bind itself to the US.

In many ways, the US was a long work in creation. Its revolution of 1776 only allowed for a Presidency of the sort with which we are now familiar in 1789; and it was only in that year that a Bill of Rights was adopted or, rather, 12 of 39 proposed rights. In 1992, there was still one of the original rights outstanding. This was to do with congressional apportionment – a means of determining the size of the House of Representatives. Voting in what now declares itself the epitome of democracy was likewise far from universal, with various portions of the population excluded from the franchise right up to the 1960s. The original 'democracy' was suffrage for white adult males. It was not universal even within this group, as a small number of residual property requirements persisted until 1850, and some such requirements lingered until 1966. Black people had to wait until 1870 and the civil war that followed. Women had to wait till 1920, and native Americans until 1924. The inhabitants of the District of Columbia could not vote in Presidential elections until 1961. Apart from the franchise, full political rights in many parts of the US were denied to black people until the civil rights movement of the 1960s, and race remains a great divider in the country today. The McCarthy anti-Communist witch-hunts of the 1950s denied civil liberties to many white people too.

If domestic politics were slow in their development of the received image of the US, foreign policy was also a slow act of creation. Despite its declaration of independence, the fledgling US still had to navigate diplomatic obstacles placed in its path by Britain. Many European powers were reluctant to grant recognition. France, because of its antipathy to Britain, but also because French officers such as Lafayette served alongside the US anti-colonial forces, granted recognition in 1777. This was followed by a formal military alliance in 1778. But, with echoes of Queen Elizabeth I, who had been faced with huge diplomatic and political antagonism from Catholic Spain, and who then received the Moroccan ambassador at her court, it was Morocco who became the first state after France to offer recognition in 1778. The offer came with a literal price. In effect, it was an extortion. If the US paid Morocco a certain sum, Morocco would both recognise the US and ensure its corsairs and pirates did not attack US shipping.

The relationship between a formal state and pirate fleets, willing to sell their services to a parent state, was then common. The Chinese emperor engaged pirate admirals as mercenary officers to defeat the Dutch in Formosa (today's Taiwan), and probably to keep the kingdom of Okinawa a Chinese as opposed to Japanese vassal. Andrew Jackson himself employed the military help of pirate captain Jean Lafitte in the defence of New Orleans in the renewed hostilities with the British in 1812.

For the remainder of the 1700s, however, the US – while slowly receiving diplomatic recognitions – was paying ransoms or negotiating ransoms with North African states to restrain their pirate fleets. Finally, by 1800, it all became too much when the Tripolitan government (in what is now Libya) raised its asking price. Very much as a precaution against what were called the 'Barbary pirates' of Algiers, Morocco, Tripoli and Tunis, the US had begun building six frigates in 1794. It was the birth of the US navy. In 1800 it blockaded Tripoli. By this time Tripoli had declared war against the US and, in 1802, Morocco followed suit. In 1803, the US sent forces that landed in Tripoli, the first such military incursion by the US on the other side of the Atlantic and, in 1805, the US finalised plans for regime change in Tripoli and an army of US marines and mercenaries landed near the city. Last minute diplomacy averted regime change – but a new stage had been set, in which US forces and military technology entered the wider world.

But that wider world for the most part was the American land mass in the 1800s, as the US increased its geographical size by either war or economic agreements with other states. A lot of this concerned Latin America – and the international image of the 'brash yankee' was born. In fact the Monroe Doctrine of 1823 deliberately warned off European powers from interventionist foreign policies in Latin America. The region was now a US zone of security, and effectively a sphere of influence. The first century of US diplomacy was to do with expansion and consolidation in terms of land. The 1803 Louisiana Purchase (from France) doubled the size of the US (Louisiana having different borders then); Spain ceded Florida in 1819; Texas was annexed in 1845, and the role of US militias – of the sort involving Davy Crocket at the Alamo – was a feature of an occupation and seizure; the end of the war with Mexico in 1848 brought California, Arizona and New Mexico into the US; Alaska was purchased from Russia in 1867; it annexed Hawaii in 1898; and victory in the war with Spain in 1898 brought vast influence over the Philippines, Puerto Rico, and Cuba. Guantanamo Bay came under US jurisdiction in 1903.

The US was not averse to using unofficial militias. Blackwater had predecessors. Theodore Roosevelt's 'Rough Riders', in the days before he became President, storming across Cuba in 1898, were reported in the US as heroic and swashbuckling. It certainly made Roosevelt's reputation as a man of action. It is fair to say that the US took quite some time to settle into being a Westphalian state, observing the limits of action against other Westphalian states. One might think that this sense of elbowing around the American region would have died away in the 20th century, especially with the election of the idealistic and cerebral Woodrow Wilson. This was not the case. In the years leading up to 1918 there were US troops in Nicaragua, the Dominican Republic, and Haiti. Wilson made an unsuccessful effort to intervene in Mexico in 1913. He famously said, "I am going to teach the South American Republics to elect good men."[7] The sense of a combined regional hegemony and a superior sense of democratic values – even when they were undemocratically imposed – was a feature of both US self-regard and its regard for the external world. When, as noted in the last chapter, after World War I and the peace negotiations in which Wilson participated, he described his (immense) contribution in the words, "at last the world knows America as the saviour of the world," an idealism and a conceit had entered international relations.

That contribution, as we noted in the previous chapter, inspired the foundation of the academic discipline, International Relations. But Wilson had also led the US into World War I, becoming the tipping point that finally defeated Germany. *The New York Times* of 3 April 1917 carried a banner headline, "President calls for War Declaration, Stronger Navy, New Army of 500,000 Men, Full Co-operation with Germany's Foes". His idealism was accompanied by a sense of power and its projection. This was not only in Latin America and in the European war, but the vocation of power was cynically reluctant to recognise the rights of struggling emergent states – and China, though huge and heir to a vast history, was having great difficulty, precisely because of the weight of its heritage, in emerging into the modern world. US troops participated in the suppression of the Chinese Boxer Uprising in the early 1900s. In 1917 the US, under the Lansing-Ishii Agreement, recognised Japan's claim to special interests in China – which was a way of recognising the reality of Japan's expansionism in China and its developing strategy of client governments. In the years after Wilson, under Franklin Roosevelt, the US was more sympathetic to China as Japan expanded dramatically into Chinese territory and committed atrocities – but war against Japan awaited the 1941 attack on Pearl Harbour by the Japanese air-force and the sinking of a huge number of largely defenceless US warships. It was in fact World War II that saw the US finally achieve the apotheosis of its earlier posturings and conceits and become a world superpower.

Germany and Italy declared war on the US shortly after Pearl Harbour, so the US became a full-scale belligerent in World War II. But, even before then, Roosevelt had enunciated his Four Freedoms – from want and fear, and of

---

[7]   Statement of 1913. See Paul Horgan, *Great River: the Rio Grande in North American History*, Middletown: Wesleyan University Press, 1984, p 913.

freedom of speech and religion – and brought them to the Anglo-American summit near Newfoundland where the Atlantic Charter was signed, a document of freedoms and idealism which became the normative purpose for fighting the war. The US became a leading player in that war, and took its place as one of the major powers in summits of allied leaders in Casablanca, Moscow, Cairo, Tehran, Bretton Woods, Yalta and Potsdam, which both plotted the course of war and, essentially the disposition and division of the world afterwards. The San Francisco conference, shortly after Germany's surrender, established the United Nations – with its Security Council, and thus its capacity to conduct diplomacy by concert, while the greater congress of member states occupied the General Assembly.

Above all, however, the war ended with the US possessing nuclear weapons. It had acquired, and deployed over Nagasaki and Hiroshima, what remains the ultimate military power a state can exercise in the pursuit of its interests.

In addition, after the war, through the Marshall Plan, the US used its economic might to rebuild Western Europe. This was as much to have a developed bulwark against communism as a concern for Europe in itself. But it also allowed the US immense leverage on the trans-Atlantic trade that followed, and gave markets to US industries which had grown immensely during the war; the race to produce armaments and machinery had doubled US industrial production and the economy had roared forward as a result. The US largesse did not extend to the rebuilding of the Soviet Union, whose immense sacrifices during World War II remained under-appreciated for a very long time. But it must have seemed to the Soviets that an immense machinery of confrontation was being built on its doorstep. It was itself struggling to rebuild, and to achieve some form of equivalence with the US in terms of nuclear weaponry. The Cold War that began almost as soon as World War II ended might perhaps have been avoided, or been less chill, if some sort of inclusiveness had been extended to the Soviet Union. Instead, the blockade of Berlin by the Soviets, and the airlift of relief by the West, during 1948-9, offered a glimpse of a future in which confrontations over nuclear missiles in Cuba became perhaps inevitable. NATO was formed in 1949. The Cold War rapidly became hot, not directly against the Soviet Union, but against its communist partner, China, and its allies. Conflict in Korea and then Vietnam embroiled the US in ground warfare that cost it many young men who came of age in the post-World War II generation.

And Latin America never went away from the long list of US global concerns. It, like the Middle East and North Africa, where US foreign policy and efforts at diplomacy and regime change began, remained a site of intervention. As mentioned earlier, the Bay of Pigs invasion of Cuba in 1961 preceded the

Cuban missile crisis. As late as 1983, the US invaded Grenada and effected regime change there, even though Maurice Bishop's government of the tiny Caribbean state, while rhetorically left-wing, was in no position at all to threaten the US.

The new Barbary pirates after the Cold War

The demise of communism after 1989, despite philosophical rhetoric of the 'end of history' and the victory of democratic liberalism, nevertheless left the world's now sole-superpower with both a foreign policy and military planning apparatus geared towards confrontation with an enemy. Being alone and on top did not suit a US with developed traditions, practices and forms of operational readiness that required a threat or a competitor. To an extent, foreign policy had to begin the discovery of threats, or the elevation of those that had taken second place behind the Soviets. And it had to accord the new threats the same kind of organisational attributes as the old one. 'Repertoire' responses were in fact reinforced in the absence of desirable threats, and little real imagination went into the contemplation of threats that were unorthodox or that could not be met by the repertoire.

The US did not have long to wait for the appearance of an underwhelming Iraq and its invasion of Kuwait. By 'underwhelming' I mean that Iraq posed no possible threat to the US, and even Kuwait's petroleum resources were unlikely to be sold to many other people – the US, in any case, being able to shift to other suppliers with a minimum of disruption. A genuine case existed for the defence of a state within the Westphalian system – even though Kuwait was an artefact of the division of the Middle East plotted by the British and French after World War I; it could just as well have been part of Iraq. But the invasion disturbed the regional balance of power – not as it has been often expressed, between Sunni and Shi'a nations, but within the Sunni nations themselves. Saudi Arabia did not take kindly to an expansion of Iraqi territory, income and capacity. The interesting thing is that neither did Iraq's ideological bed-fellow, Syria. Both Iraq and Syria had been led into the modern post-war world by the secular Ba'ath party. They had characteristics in common, which included national development goals that were technological, areligious and, within dictatorial systems of government, inclined towards the modern development of women. Yet Syria came to the side of the great coalition that assembled, under US leadership, to expel Iraq from Kuwait. Here, the foreign policies of the regional Arab states were uniformly cognisant of

1. The fact that their own statehoods and borders were recent and, in the case of Syria and its war with Israel, not fully secure. There was therefore

a genuine Westphalian impulse at work.

2. The US was now a world hegemon, but even a hegemon needed conspicuously visible and willing allies, but the fragility of alliances and partnerships was revealed in the case of Iraq from 1980 to 1988. In the 1980s Iraq was encouraged by the US, and financed by both the US and Saudi Arabia, to wage war on revolutionary Iran. Having used Iraq then, its services and its leadership could be jettisoned later. The new hegemon could be fickle if its rules of operation were transgressed, and those rules saw the need for state behaviour and diplomacy along Westphalian lines – at least in those areas where the US did not itself deploy non-Westphalian interventions.

3. Finally, there might be financial rewards in the venture. Armies could be restocked and equipment upgraded in a joint operation of the size contemplated in Kuwait.

How the US felt about such considerations is not fully clear. However, it was a considerable diplomatic feat to put together the extensive militarised coalition that assembled against Iraq. It was the first, and last, time the US managed something like this. The later war in Afghanistan involved NATO forces as allies, and others who had always been in the Western camp. The Syrians and other Arab states were conspicuously absent in Gulf War II that set about not the defence of a Westphalian state but regime change within a recognised member of the Westphalian system – something that even a major Western power, France, found difficult to support.

Why the change from the Westphalian restraint of the US under George Bush in Gulf War I, 1990 – where he conspicuously ordered coalition forces not to advance on Baghdad and withdraw to liberated Kuwait – to Gulf War II in 2003, little over a decade later, with the determination of George W. Bush and the British prime Minister, Tony Blair, to advance with shock and awe on Baghdad? Tony Blair's approach, as we shall discuss later, was couched in a desire to be seen as one with the world's hegemonic power – an offset to Britain's otherwise diminished world position; but the mood in the US, highly supportive of military interventionism, especially against a 'proven' enemy from Gulf War I, did benefit from a huge discursive shift within the US. In a way, the US is a real case example for the Copenhagen School's approach to the discursive foundations of foreign policy formulation. Samuel Huntington's lecture of 1992, his *Foreign Affairs* article based on the lecture,[8] and his 1996 book based on the article, *The Clash of Civilizations*,[9] had a tremendously

---

8   Samuel P. Huntington, 'The Clash of Civilizations?', *Foreign Affairs*, Summer 1993.

9   Samuel P. Huntington, *The Clash of Civilizations and the Remaking of World Order*,

evocative and provocative effect on US debate. The contention that the world was once again divided, that the division was antagonistic, and that US foreign policy should be protective of itself, and that this protection should effectively be against an internationalised Islamic fundamentalism were all read into the book, and certainly featured in the debate it generated. When, in September 2001, the Twin Towers were attacked in New York, the US once more had a military enemy. It had a state from which it emanated, and that was Afghanistan – even though the organisation that perpetrated the attack, Al Qaeda, was simultaneously a trans-state and non-state entity. US and NATO forces invaded Afghanistan before 2001 was out and easily seized the capital city, Kabul.

The crafting of a diabolical image of the new enemies – the Taliban as repressive and joyless; Al Qaeda as sinister and sneaky as well as internationally subversive; and Iraq as being led by a genocidal dictator with weapons of mass destruction and obvious mass outreach with those weapons – proceeded apace. They were the new Barbary Pirates of the new millennium: extortionate, treacherous, threatening and very different. Insofar as such images also entered public discourse – and President George W. Bush ensured they were part of official discourse with his 'axis of evil' speech – they may have helped configure foreign policy, if even in a crude sense, but did nothing for the sophistication of that policy. This of course is the essential difficulty of the Copenhagen School – not that discourse does not form, but what kind of thing it helps to form with what kind of discourse is also something very much at stake. We shall see, when it comes to US foreign policy towards the Middle East, it has helped to form something far from helpful to the safety of the region and the wider world.

The US has always been pivotal to the Middle East. Woodrow Wilson did not object to the Balfour Declaration that proposed the division of Palestine into a Jewish state and a Palestinian one; but the US did object to the Anglo-French-Israeli effort to seize the Suez Canal in 1956 after Egypt nationalised it, and effectively forced the invading armies to withdraw. It was Henry Kissinger who sought to establish a balance of power between Egypt and Israel in the wake of their hostilities, and did this by liberal military aid to both – but more so in the case of Israel. The balance of power would be, in this way, always slightly tilted in Israel's favour. For a long time, Israel and Egypt were the two largest recipients of US military aid – but, by 2010, the disbursal of such aid favoured firstly Iraq (with $6.5 billion), then Afghanistan ($5.6 billion), with Israel third ($2.75 billion) and Egypt fourth ($1.75 billion).

Pakistan was fifth ($1.6 billion). This was about a third of the total foreign aid

New York: Simon & Schuster, 1996.

budget of about $40 billion. It has done little to ensure the Iraqi armed forces can stand before ISIS, the Afghanistani armed forces can stand in the face of a resurgent Taliban, or the Pakistani armed forces can overcome their own version of the Taliban. It has certainly ensured that Israel holds all military advantages in the ongoing struggle against Palestinian aspirations for statehood. But financing proxies may never have been enough, and one of the great vexed questions of US foreign policy under the Obama administration has been how much to wind down, or wind up, direct US military involvement in theatres such as Afghanistan, Iraq and Syria.

Diplomacy and the Chinese dragon

Napoleon spoke of China as a sleeping giant, and that the world should beware its awakening. The world spent a long time trying to keep the dragon asleep or restrained. What the Chinese call an era of unequal treaties and humiliation was forced upon the country by the Western powers and Japan. It was Japan in particular that forcibly occupied Manchuria and later swept by force of arms into other parts of China, leading up to and within World War II. The divided Chinese governments and armies for the most part could not stand against the technologically driven Japanese forces with their modern arms, better generalship, and military ruthlessness. The US provided some help and outreach to Mao's communist armies, but by far the bulk of US assistance went to Chiang Kai Shek's nationalist forces. When they were defeated in 1949, and forced to retreat to Taiwan, the victorious communist regime was diplomatically ostracised by the US and deprived of its seat on the UN Security Council. That went to the rump nationalist government on Taiwan, and Taiwan was itself guarded by the US 7th fleet. Diplomatically and militarily, China and the US were in a state of confrontation. That became bloody as the two powers supported North and South Korea in the war of the early 1950s, and did so with their armed forces and without much quarter asked or given.

It was Henry Kissinger and Richard Nixon who, anxious not only to exit the Vietnam war, but to do so without disadvantage in the Cold War against the Soviet Union – where every defeat could be seen as a humiliation – devised a *rapprochement* with China in 1971-2. This would strengthen China in its own quarrel with the Soviet Union, which had led the two former communist allies to a bitter ideological and political rivalry, and would give a sense of orderly and calculated behaviour in Asia, rather than an unscripted retreat from a war where the US had bombed North Vietnam with massive airpower, but had still not defeated its will to attack the south and unify the country.

Although the Vietnam war wound down only with huge militarised manoeuvres and actions, the *rapprochement* with China was, in a way, US diplomacy at its most sophisticated: not dictated by values or ideology, and not predicated on military power or economic purchase in the direction of China. It was an alliance of convenience that, with one stroke, added pressure upon the Soviet Union in its quarrel with a China no longer having to worry about a US threat, and stabilised the Asian theatre with a China who would feel more secure from no longer being in diplomatic isolation; and behave, Kissinger calculated, more responsibly – and it did. It also brought China, finally given its seat on the Security Council, into the world concert of great powers – where it would be obliged, even at the level of great states, to obey certain Westphalian conventions rather than continue a default into antagonism.

But, if the US could deal well with such a case – and it must be said the Chinese reciprocated Kissinger's sophistication with their own – the same could not always be said of US foreign policy and diplomacy in the Middle East, particularly where they concerned belligerent non-state actors. We shall follow that in later chapters. For now, the relationship between Britain and the US deserves some comment.

The tail that wants the dog to wag it

As the Cold War began, Britain helped the US and other Western allies to run the Soviet blockade of West Berlin – airlifting vital supplies to the population in 1948-9. It also fought alongside the US in the Korean war of 1950-3. But the other British efforts, outside its US partnership, were not always glorious or successful. The creation of Israel, with a British mandate until independence, 1945-8, was marked by violence and terrorism and UN complaints that the British were not cooperative in the transition period. The Malayan emergency, 1948-60, with British forces embroiled in jungle warfare against communist insurgents, was 'successful' but led to accusations of heavy-handedness and atrocity. Most of all, as noted earlier, the intervention in Suez in 1956, and the chastisement from the US, led to a withdrawal with the British tail firmly between its legs. It all led to the period, 1964-8, and the British withdrawal from Malaysia and Singapore – what was called the cessation of international power projection 'east of Suez'. Britain became a North Atlantic state, increasingly concerned with Europe and how to manage an asymmetrical relationship with the much more powerful US.

The British were the instigators in persuading the US, through the CIA, to help overthrow the Iranian government for the sake of their oil interests in 1953, but otherwise – Suez aside - undertook no really significant foreign policy interventions – except fishery disputes with Iceland (the 'cod wars') –

until 1979, when the independence of Zimbabwe was finally negotiated after years of hesitation and indecision; and 1982, when war broke out with Argentina over the Falkland Islands. Although hailed, in Britain, as a great military triumph, the war had been a near-run thing. If more of the Argentinian French-made Exocet missiles had exploded when they hit their targets, sufficient ships in the British fleet may have been sunk for the cost to have become too great – forcing a British withdrawal. Otherwise, the 1980s were characterised by British reluctance to join a sanctions campaign against Apartheid South Africa; and quarrels with Libya, especially when a Pan Am flight exploded over Scotland in 1988 – with the finger of suspicion pointing at Libya. But outside Northern Ireland, against the IRA insurrection there, no British military intervention occurred until the 1990s when suddenly, as part of multilateral efforts, Britain was called upon to play armed and belligerent roles. These were Gulf War I, as part of the coalition against Iraq in 1991; and as part of the NATO bombing campaign in the Yugoslav war over Kosovo and Belgrade in 1999.

Britain was part of the 2001 military intervention in Afghanistan after 9/11 – but its only solo military effort in this period was to defend Freetown in Sierra Leone against rebel assault in 2000, and subsequently drive the rebel forces towards defeat. Everything else was as part of joint operations and all of these bore the leadership imprint of the US – especially in Gulf War II, when Britain allied itself closely with the US-led invasion of Iraq in 2003. 46,000 British soldiers were eventually involved. The public reaction against such involvement, and the casualties involved – especially when it became clearer that Iraq might, after all, have possessed no 'weapons of mass destruction' able to reach Western shores - has meant that in the subsequent campaigns in Libya, Iraq and Syria involved only warplanes. Indeed, all the participating Western forces were reluctant to be drawn into ground combat.

But the alacrity with which British Prime Minister Tony Blair came to the side of US President George W. Bush over the Iraq issue bears some comment. It was not impulsive or desperate. In a real sense, Blair acted according to Churchill's post-war diagnosis that the UK faced three concentric circles that marked its future: closeness to the US; closeness to Europe; and closeness to the Commonwealth. Churchill understood that the weakened UK had no real choice but to commit itself to a trans-Atlantic alliance with the US. At the same time, the US was building a new Europe with redevelopment finance on a grand scale. The reality was not in fact that there were three circles, but that they were concentric circles. How you handled the overlaps, and how much of each overlap you allowed at any one moment in time, was key. Where Blair seemed to act rashly was his readiness to move only with the US, ignoring for instance the concerns of France as a major European partner. Even so, Blair's commitment to the notion that any UK projection of power in international politics could only work if it was in concert with the power of the US, could seem slavish – or it could seem a rational calculation on the possibilities of a concert of two. One way or another, the UK saw a 'special relationship' with the US as key to its future in the globe. It was a special relationship with a manifestly stronger and more powerful state. Allying oneself with its power also meant an adherence to its interests – or at least declaring a commonality of interests, which is what the UK did over the Iraq issue.

The fallout from siding so readily with the US over the invasion of Iraq has been such that any future UK adherence to US power projection of this sort seems unlikely. The UK has had to act with both the US and the EU over Russian expansionism into Ukraine and the annexation of Crimea; it has had to negotiate with Europe over the Transatlantic Trade and Investment Partnership with the US; it has had to watch as China announced huge investments in the UK, but even greater ones in Europe, but clearly seeing each as interconnected with the other. There is no longer a semblance of an autonomous foreign policy – and the much vaunted 'Rolls Royce' machine of the Foreign Office and its diplomatic prowess now seeks to eke out influence rather than power.

Two meditations

One

As we shall see in the chapters to come, the US sense of being a sole hegemonic power, a lone superpower, is under challenge – even as it patiently and indulgently pulls along the UK and allows it to think of the relationship as special. It may be that the day is dawning when the US itself will seek membership of a genuine multilateralism – of which it is not automatically the leader or the most powerful member. As Russia sets about its resurgence, as China grows into the world's strongest economic force, and as it fields an array of trading and financial institutions in all parts of the world – both of which will be discussed in later chapters – the US may have set about its own quest for Trans-Atlantic or Trans-Pacific Trade and Investment regimes a little later in the day than was wise. The Kissinger-led *rapprochement* with China, among other things, gave China space and the sense of security in which to grow. How swiftly it grew surprised many.

Two

The UK, most visibly and lacking in subtlety under Prime Minister Blair, worked assiduously at asserting a special relationship with the US and did so by being highly supportive of controversial US foreign policy initiatives – such as the invasion of Iraq. Two things were at work here. The first was a determination, almost a desperation, to appear to be able to project power as a state – even if under another's more powerful cloak.

The second was the historical British imagination of its international interests – which was required to be maintained by the projection of power – insofar as that was possible. This imagination was based on a memory of its interests, as they seemed to be before the withdrawal east of Suez, and before the debacle of the invasion of the Suez Canal zone itself in 1956. In this sense, the English School of International Relations amasses much credence – that a view of the international is historically formed, almost determined, and this impacts upon foreign policy formulation and diplomatic practice, even if the posture that results seems absurd.

The US has indulged this British conceit, but in the Babylonian king's dream the rock of Heaven strikes the feet of the statue because they were made of materials that never genuinely bonded together. Power ebbs and flows – and flows away.

3

The Rise and Fall of Europe: Unity and Challenge

The idea of Europe was grand, but also gradual. The project of rebuilding after World War II was shared, and the US Marshall Plan was of huge importance, but the sense was also of Europe needing to do something organisationally for itself, and to do it in a unified form. From this, the idea of unity as an overarching goal began to develop. But the first steps were very specific ones. They began with the formation of the European Coal and Steel Community in 1951. Unity and cooperation in this sector were clearly necessary for the industrial redevelopment of Europe – but theorists began to read such steps of 'functional cooperation' as preconditions for wider cooperation, and formal regimes of cooperation.

From the start there was a triptych of organisational methods – beginning with harmonisation, then cooperation, and finally a regime of coordination. It is this last stage that Europe has now reached, and it is this that has caused grave disquiets among many member states who see the coordinating bureaucracy and regulatory frameworks of Brussels as having intruded upon national sovereignty in the old Westphalian sense of sovereign states having sovereign public administrations serving sovereign constitutions and laws. This was very much the essence of debate in the UK, as it underwent its 2016 referendum on continued membership – the extent to which sovereignty had been eroded by a coordinating machinery in Brussels, which was not answerable to a UK electorate, or even any electorate.

The triptych of harmonisation, cooperation and coordination was not designed as a progressive one. It was simply a means to analyse types of inter-governmental organisation. Harmonisation is to do with common principles, including in the case of the OECD, common principles of economic planning and behaviour. Cooperation is to do with states agreeing a joint venture, or a float of ventures, but it is still the states who call the shots, even if they have a secretariat in common for those ventures. Coordination, however, is very much the realm of a supra-state body that keeps the participating states in line with treaty agreements which have the status and power of law.

The tension in the growth of the European Union, between steps of increasingly functional cooperation, spreading from the coal and steel sector to others, but always centred on technical functionality – and the grand vision of statesmen like Jean Monnet, who in fact had been in charge precisely of coal and steel, but had also in an astounding precocity been Deputy Secretary-General of the League of Nations at age 31, that envisaged a new European economic order and, finally, a European political union – haunted the growth of the Union as it passed through its treaty phases, the provisions of each treaty being adopted into national laws.

The Treaty of Rome in 1957 created what was then called the European Economic Community, and it might be said that the founding intent was not yet fully political. By the time of the 1993 Maastricht Treaty, the European Union had a firm economic mission and political intent. Europe absorbed a range of sovereign powers from its members in order to achieve a functional and public administrative commonality of standards and procedures for all members. A member state like the UK negotiated an 'opt out' of some of these commonalities, but for the majority of the states in the EU, the commonality of European standards and procedures is either an aspirational or achieved reality.

There are, however, two particular aspects of the European project which bear note – one is a note of pronounced concern for certain members, such as Greece, and that is to do with economic and fiscal policy; and the other strikes a note of very great concern for neighbouring Russia, and that is a European common security policy which has no choice but to achieve its operationalisation through NATO.

The bank

Membership of the EU does not oblige a state to join either the European Bank or the Eurozone. However 19 of the 28 member states did join the Eurozone, which was created in 1999, with the European Bank having been created in 1998, both to manage the Euro and to act as a provider of liquidity under negotiated conditionalities and fiscal regimes. The problem was that there was a common currency without a common fiscal policy – except insofar as the receipt of liquidity created a fiscal zone dictated by Europe; either by the Bank itself or by European leaders acting through the Bank and, often, in concert with other lending agencies such as the International Monetary Fund (IMF).

Even states that were not part of the Eurozone, but whose debts and trading relationships were demarcated in Euros, found their national economic conditions and outlooks heavily influenced if not determined by the value of the Euro and policy decisions of the Bank. The sheer weight of Euro reserves and capacity also made the currency and the Bank impossible to avoid. The Euro is the world's second largest reserve currency, and there are more Euros in international circulation than US dollars.

Thus, almost all European states, in one way or another, were caught up in the Greek financial crisis that peaked in 2015. Total European Bank and IMF bailout funds for Greece were Euro 110 billion, a huge sum to be outstanding even against the combined liquidities and reserves of European states – themselves for the most part still recovering from the banking crisis of 2008.

What the Greeks found was that they no longer had any fiscal sovereignty of their own. The conditionalities of the bailout meant an austerity almost no sovereign government, answerable to an electorate and public opinion, would by itself impose. The Greek situation was unique, in that few other European states could contrive to mismanage their economies to such an extent, and require the assistance of so many billions. However, the situation was illustrative of a fundamental European reality. Even if political union is still resisted and contested, the economy of Europe is increasingly being seen as a single unit. It is not yet a fully coherent unit, and independent parts of it, e.g. the British and German economies, still have huge command on their own – but they have still greater command and international economic leverage together.

Security

Europe has external security threats, but also those closer to home – or within the precinct of home. Two current member states, against one hoping to become a member, were at war as recently as 1991-8. These were the Yugoslav wars, in which Slovenia and Croatia were at war with Serbia. The question of Kosovo, a country that achieved a highly contested independence from Serbia in 2008, is being 'managed', but is not resolved; and nor is the future of a bitterly divided Bosnia, with its Serbian enclave administrations, and which was the site of the terrible siege of Sarajevo – at its worst a throwback to the medieval assaults against cities by strangulation and slaughter.

The European Union does have a Common Foreign and Security Policy. It has a Foreign Affairs Council and a High Representative, a ministerial-type figure who acts as spokesperson on joint European foreign policy. Part of the overall apparatus, since 1999, is the Common Security and Defence Policy. It has very limited military capability and, basically, the specifically European and EU-related security mechanisms extend as far as forms of peacekeeping. For actual military projection, the EU depends upon an intimate association with NATO. The relationship between the two organisations has been described as "separable but not separate",[10] and the ratification of the Lisbon treaty in 2007 virtually merged the European security system with NATO. It was NATO forces that were involved in the end-games of the Yugoslav wars over Kosovo. Aspiring members of the EU, all now from the old East European buffer and Warsaw Pact states, under the Eastern partnership programme, if they are to sign an Association Agreement with the EU, must make a deliberate and articulated choice between maintaining close ties with Russia and integration with the EU. A state cannot have both. What this means is not only integration with the EU, but an accommodation if not association with NATO. From a Russian perspective, this can only seem threatening; the mobilisation of an oppositional bloc.

Europe also has an anti-terrorism policy. It has a list of designated terrorist organisations. It is far from an exact list. One of the listed organisations, the Kurdish PKK, is in fact a military ally of NATO in the war against ISIS. Its presence on the list is largely a sop to Turkey, who certainly regards the PKK's quest for Kurdish independence – or even autonomy – as a terrorist threat. Turkey has long sought some kind of closer link to the EU, if not eventual membership.

The list is one thing. Doing something about it is another. And the very existence of a list presupposes, somewhat naively, that terrorism proceeds via formal organisation – whereas a group that functions via secret and separate cells is something very different. Keeping track of such cells, or even knowing about them, certainly defeated Belgium's fractured security agencies before the attacks on Brussels in 2016; and earlier did not provide warning to France that the same cells would attack Paris in 2015. Al Qaeda was not even on the list for some time. It, ISIS, and other terrorist outfits almost certainly smile at the European bureaucratic endeavour to counter terrorism.

However, an area where European unity has been very important is

---

[10]   Formulation from the December 1999 EU summit in Helsinki. See Nora Bensahel, ' "Separable but not separate" – NATO's development of the combined joint task force', *European Security*, 8:2, 2007.

humanitarian assistance. The European Community Humanitarian Aid Office, devotes about Euro 1 billion in annual emergency aid. Together with the contributions of individual member states, the combined humanitarian emergency capacity is greater than anything else on earth.

Russia

After the 9/11 attacks Russia moved swiftly to support the US in its War on Terror. It was both a genuine solidarity against terrorism and an olive branch that sought a special relationship with the leading power within NATO. The US sought almost pointedly to repudiate the Russian gesture. It withdrew from the 1972 Anti-Ballistic Missile Treaty in 2001, and chose to proceed with the expansion of NATO right up to Russia's frontiers in 2002. Since 2003, when Russia declined to support the invasion of Iraq, relations between the US/NATO and Russia have cooled.

President Putin made his position very clear in a landmark speech, made in Munich, in February 2007.[11] He strongly weighed against the US's seeming desire to be monopolistic in its dominance of world affairs and its "almost uncontained hyper use of force in international relations". It had the opposite of its intended result, in that "no one feels safe!" No one felt they could be guaranteed protection by international law. As a result, the US posture could only stimulate a new arms race. Putin called for an inclusive "fair and democratic world order that would ensure security and prosperity not only for a select few, but for all." The speech was, in short, a protest against not being included in the kind of world order envisaged by the US, but it was also against the expansionism of NATO which certainly did not make Russia feel safe. The pointed warning about a new arms race was a declaration of a new pro-activity of Russia in world politics.

This determination was reinforced by NATO action in Kosovo and in the EU's involvement in the independence of Kosovo in 2008 – greatly antagonising Serbia, which had long seen Russia as an ally. But Putin's language over Kosovo was carefully crafted to serve as a defence of Westphalian statehood, i.e. against secession from recognised states, in this case from Serbia. It was, Putin said, both immoral and illegal, but was a "terrible precedent" that would begin to destroy the system of international relations developed over centuries.[12] It was almost as if, taking the Western cue, Putin was forecasting his own annexation of Crimea some years in the future.

---

[11]   https://www.youtube.com/watch?v=ZlY5aZfOgPA
[12]   See report in the *Sydney Morning herald*, 23 February 2008.

The noted Russia observer, Richard Sakwa, argues that the EU's approach to Ukraine as part of its version of a 'Wider Europe', effectively excluded Russia from all Western European regional cooperation structures.[13] Putin wanted a 'Greater Europe', in which all had equal rights and opportunities, including Russia. The Russian view was that the end of the Cold War was in fact a shared victory. It was a victory for a peaceful future. The West, in insisting it had won the Cold War, in its triumphalism, treated Russia instead as a defeated enemy and set about trying to marginalise it in plans for a greater EU/NATO zone.

The floral and colour revolutions – the Rose Revolution in Georgia (2003), the Orange Revolution in Ukraine (2004), and the Tulip Revolution in Kyrgyzstan (2005) – led Russia to a realm of great caution, if not paranoia as to how these political changes would be exploited by the West. Early indications that Georgia and Ukraine would seek membership of NATO (abandoned by Ukraine in 2010) stoked this paranoia. But, in this context, war in Georgia and effective annexation of two Georgian provinces by Russia in 2008; and the formal annexation of Crimea in 2014, up till then part of Ukraine, meant a Russia intent of rolling back what it perceived to be the encroaching borders both of the EU and NATO.

An extended meditation

After the fall of Communism and the end of the Soviet Union, the US entered a public phase of triumphalism. It delighted in being a sole superpower and a solo hegemon. However, under the surface, none of its foreign policy and defence procedures changed. They were all calibrated on the existence of a powerful enemy. Enemies of the most enigmatic sort duly appeared, and the 'War on Terror' that resulted had as its early hallmark the felt need to invade two states, Afghanistan and Iraq. It was states that could be attacked. The designation of an 'axis of evil' was accomplished by naming a number of states. It was as if US state interests, and the projection of US state power could only be calculated and executed against other states. But this did not defeat terrorism at all. And, while the US struggled to find a conceptualisation of terror and its organisation, its policy machine was thankful that Russia began its resurgence and could, once again assume its place as an antagonist power.

In short, the resurgence of Russia rehabilitated a range of repertoire responses – as they were produced and refined by a number of government departments and their organisational procedures and processes. In a real

---

[13]   Richard Sakwa, *Frontline Ukraine: Crisis in the Borderlands*, London: I.B. Tauris, 2014.

way of course, it was easier than when the Soviet Union was a genuine superpower. The Russia of the new millennium was a weakened version of what went before. However, it had sufficient characteristics in common with the 'old model' that old model responses could be wheeled out by the US foreign policy machine.

It also allowed the maintenance and development of military spending levels, and technological investments. Unlike terrorist organisations, Russia still had modern warplanes, warships, and nuclear missiles. These had to be matched and superseded. In this way, an entire industrial support base – and its economic importance to the US – what used to be called the 'military-industrial complex', could be retained and expanded.

Defence industries and a Department of Defence that was strong also meant the maintenance of internal 'balances of power' between government departments in Washington DC – notably between Defence and the Department of State. The *status quo* of Washington's political dispositions towards the outside world was as before.

In a way, foreign policy formulation is necessarily dyadic. It begins with an 'us' and an 'out there', towards which policy is directed. It allows the use of methodologies like game theory to calibrate competitive interests, power, values, and rational responses. Only with an enemy in one's own image can game theory and 'scientific' and predictive foreign policy work. In a very real sense, in the US it was 'welcome back, Russia! We missed you.'

For Europe, however, the picture should have been different. A union of states that sought, even if it never achieved, some sort of political commonality, nevertheless was anchored on a genuine sense of multilateralism. There was a huge functional base to the European project which by the new millennium went way beyond coal and steel. The foundational sense of functional cooperation might perhaps have dictated a need to establish a cooperative regime with Russia in the area of natural gas – both Germany as well as Ukraine depending on Russian natural gas every single winter. From functional cooperation, as the early theorists of Europe hoped, political cooperation could grow. Russia, with its sense of the end of the Cold War being a shared victory, and not a cause of triumphalism for one side only, might have welcomed steps towards political cooperation – even if it could not be intimate cooperation. But what happened was an indication of the limits of multilateralism, in that –finally – ideological and political history do get in the way of functionalism and the reach of multilateralism. The continued existence of NATO, now once again able to have exactly the same enemy as before, and to use all of its own repertoire responses in the face of this enemy

– despite an array of signals from the enemy that it preferred not to be an enemy any more – meant a Europe, dependent on NATO as its security arm, unable to respond to Russian overtures for a new start.

Of course, should President Putin be successful in growing the Russian economy, then the EU would have an economic rival and perhaps, in a regime of cooperation, it could never have in any case entered any form of even proto-integration with something so problematic but prospectively so large. Union allows the economic domination of a small shambolic economy like Greece; it does not allow within itself two competitive monoliths. Even so, Europe may have missed an opportunity for some form of greater cooperation, and perhaps some form of greater peace on its frontiers.

4

When the Dragon Wakes

Napoleon said that the world should beware the sleeping dragon, lest it awake. In his day, China was not only asleep but lost in a time before modernity and unable to emerge from the dense dream of a bygone world – where it had been the most advanced country on earth, surely the most virtuous and wise, yet somehow it was now submerged by the power and the depredations of what were once barbarian states with primitive rulers and uncouth populations. The dragging of a somnambulant China into globalisation was a huge shock to what had become an isolated and conceited empire.

The imperial powers of the 19th century, joined by a rapidly modernising Japan, subjected China to huge humiliations that continued into the 20th century – especially on the part of Japan, who occupied much of China in the years leading up to World War II. The Chinese did not help themselves, divided into two competing armed camps with aspirations towards two very different forms of republic, a Japanese puppet administration, and several warlord enclaves. Chinese armies, no matter how desperately if belatedly they sought to modernise, fell before the Japanese because of terrible Generalship. The Nationalist Kuomintang faction, led by Chiang Kai Shek, was an official ally to the US, the UK, and the Soviet Union during the war – and fought with the British for Burma – but faced both the Japanese and the communist army of Chairman Mao back home. At the end of World War II, struggle continued in China, and the communists were victorious in 1949, driving Chiang's Nationalist forces into exile on the island of Taiwan. But China was in ruins, and the communist regime instigated its new social and economic policies at great cost to stability in the country. Diplomacy was, except with the communist Soviet Union, not a priority and, in any case, the US as ally of the defeated Nationalists was determined to freeze China out of international diplomacy and respectability.

The US, using its veto power in the Security Council of the new United Nations, prevented China from taking up its own seat on the Security Council, maintaining the rump Nationalist regime in its UN place. By 1956, even relations with the communist Soviet Union began to cool, as Nikita Khrushchev began the process of repudiating the tyrannical excesses of Stalin. To the Chinese, this was the beginning of a revisionism too far, and justified the new diplomacy to find allies in the wider world. Khrushchev became first secretary of the Soviet communist party on the death of Stalin in 1953, and there were no public indications that he would deviate significantly from the legacy he had inherited. The 25 February 1956 speech, in which – for four hours – he accused Stalin of having led a personality cult, startled the entire communist world; very much including China. But it had become clear to the Chinese even before then that relying solely on the Soviet Union for diplomatic support was unwise. In April 1955, therefore, Zhou Enlai went to the Bandung Afro-Asian conference – a huge gathering of leaders from the emerging world, and the key forerunner to the Non-Aligned Movement (NAM), and gave a landmark speech.

The diplomatic foray by Zhou, the Chinese premier, was a search for diplomatic allies and to garner international appreciation for what China had been through. Simultaneously, it was a real attempt by China to recognise that others had also gone through a century or more of horrible imperialisation. The Chinese had been so isolated from the outside world that they really had no empirical grounds for solidarity; they could not be ideological grounds, as most of the Afro-Asian world was not communist, although many countries had leanings towards one form or another of socialism; so Zhou pitched his address essentially on ethical grounds – with the insinuation of empathy. Others despoiled you. We will help you. Others imposed their sovereignty upon yours and interfered in the workings of what should have been your governments. We will never intervene in your internal affairs. The combination of assistance and non-intervention has been something the Chinese have tried to live up to, even if problematically, ever since.

In the wake of Bandung, China began its financial assistance to emerging nations – despite the Chinese communist state being only seven years old and governing a desperately poor and underdeveloped country. Chairman Mao's quick-fire jump-start schemes to hasten modernisation and industrialisation not only failed, but had huge costs in terms of social dislocation. He was a visionary poet trying to be an industrial planner, with very little knowledge of either industry or industrialisation. Those around him, like Zhou, and later Deng Xiaoping, picked up the pieces and tried to bring a pragmatic and scientific order to Chinese development. If Zhou led the way in international relations with his Bandung speech, he was also hugely influential in pioneering the concepts of the 'four modernisations', and did so as early as 1963. They were later made official policy by Mao's successor as

Chinese leader, Deng Xiaoping, in 1978. These 'modernisations' were critical to China's developing the industrial, and hence economic base that was necessary for its international relations of assistance to others – not to mention competition with the Western developed world.

Zhou also pioneered what later became the Chinese Three World Theory, described below. Although this theory was articulated as the official Chinese world view, again by Deng Xiaoping, in a speech to the United Nations in 1974, Zhou had laid down its ingredients in the 1960s. It was suitably poetic for Mao to be enthusiastic about it, and it was declared to be a formulation by Mao, in concert with the Zambian President Kenneth Kaunda, then regarded as an African 'philosopher-king', during Kaunda's visit to Beijing in 1974. It continued the themes enunciated by Zhou at Bandung. But, before 1974, the breakthrough diplomatic event that gave China the international freedom to develop its Bandung vision – the *rapprochement* with the US - took place.

Table tennis and the use of third parties

The *rapprochement* was a goal of Henry Kissinger, who wanted three things: firstly, the freedom to confront the Soviet Union as a sole superpower antagonist, without the distraction of China as another antagonist; secondly, a sense of responsible limits to Chinese regional behaviour should the US successfully exit from the Vietnam war; and, thirdly, the incorporation of China into the world's concert of great powers, both to make the concert credible and viable – with no one playing discordant notes off-stage – and to make Chinese behaviour respect the limits of being part of a concert, and therefore predictable.

For the Chinese, it was desirable. It meant China did not have to confront both the Soviet Union and the US; it meant a step towards a more peaceful region if indeed the US did resolve its interests in Vietnam; it meant being recognised, finally, as a great power – even if it meant being in a concert – and ending, officially, the epoch of humiliation; and it meant steps could be taken to achieve economic prosperity in a trading regime that did not exclude the West and, in particular, the US.

However, Kissinger had no diplomatic links directly with China at all. Moreover, US knowledge of China was limited, given the purging of linguists and Sinologists from the State Department during the McCarthy era of anti-communist witch-hunts. The Chinese were hardly in a much better position. To an extent, without organisational processes and without repertoire planning, the key roles played by Kissinger and Zhou represented the purest form of 'rational actor' behaviour seen in post-war international diplomacy –

even though, in the proper sense of the word 'rational', it must be said that the two men trusted alarmingly to intuition. Their success in being able to develop formidable personal chemistry was an accident of history. Kissinger had to use dictators for his entry point, and the Chinese had to deploy table tennis as a symbol that a new history was possible. Looking back, it was in some ways silly.

Kissinger made secret overtures in 1970 to Pakistan's Yahya Khan and Romania's Nicolae Ceausescu, the former responsible for the rebellion in East Pakistan that year and eventually its bloody secession as Bangladesh, and the latter a communist dictator certainly not mourned by the US when he was summarily executed in 1989 – and asked them to use their good offices to sound out Beijing's willingness to talk. Beijing intimated that it was willing, and then used its own subterfuge to invite US athletes to play a table tennis match in China. This happened in April 1971. In the diplomatic isolation of China after World War II, and in the ensuing era of political hostility, no such contact had ever seemed possible. It was the advent of 'Ping Pong Diplomacy', and the general sense internationally was that relations between the US and China could be unfrozen. Even so, Kissinger made two secret visits to Beijing, in July and October 1971, working with Zhou Enlai in preparation for a public visit by President Nixon to China the following year. That visit was full of pomp, but was really only the face of a *rapprochement*, the detailing of which had little to do with either Nixon or Mao. But, even though on the Chinese side it had almost everything to do with Zhou, there was as yet no full trust of the US. After so many years of hostility, there would not be an overnight transformation in foreign policy outlook. Thus, the Chinese continued work towards the Three World Theory.

The theory and its limits

The actual theory did not last long as an active conceptualisation of the world. It was as much a sentimentalism as anything else – a sense that China had a leadership role, especially amongst those who were also emerging from humiliation. The theory proposed a First World of imperial outreach and ambition, and this was a conjoint US and Soviet Union; i.e. the two great superpowers still sought global domination. The Second World was constituted by an intermediate zone, consisting in countries from Europe and, although the theory did not say so, as the Chinese never really had an articulated approach to this part of the world, from Latin America. This world could be courted by either the First or Third Worlds and success in this courtship could determine the power struggle between the First and Third. In this sense, the theory had diplomatic goals. The Third World was basically the emerging world, the Non-aligned world, but with a twist – it was a world led by

China; championed by China; protected by China.

It was this conceit, that China *could* do these things, and that other Third World states would *want* China to do these things, and that China would never do things itself against the interests of these states that, in a very short time proved false. In 1979, the Soviet Union – from 'out of a blue sky', as Western military strategists put it, i.e. without warning signs or even visible signs of preparation – invaded Afghanistan. The West could not prevent it; and nor could China. A part of the Third World had been overtaken by one half of the First – and China, far from being its effective champion and protector, could only watch, as surprised and unprepared as the West, from the sideline.

However, another significant event occurred in 1979, and this was China's own (brief) invasion of Vietnam. Having been North Vietnam's ally in the war against the US and the US-supported regime in the south, the Chinese now found themselves embroiled in conflict with the unified state it had helped to create. The invasion was brief. The Vietnamese essentially embarrassed and defeated the Chinese forces. Battle-hardened by years of struggle against the US, the Chinese were simply more of the same. But that was precisely the problem. China was behaving like a giant from the First World. It was not championing this part of the Third World at all. After 1979, the theory was never really mentioned again. This did not mean the Chinese abandoned the principle of solidarity with the emerging world. China simply realised it could not automatically be its leader. China also realised it had a lot to learn about the complexities and the ambitions of this world. Its ambitions might not coincide with Chinese ambitions; might even, in the case of the Vietnamese, run counter to Chinese ambitions.

Learning about Africa

Zhou Enlai, despite his stirring speech at Bandung, and despite his later adroit dealings with Kissinger, was far from a flawless diplomat. A visit to Africa in 1963 left him highly embarrassed as the Africans rejected his talk of revolution. It was the last thing the recently independent states sought. They sought stability.

China made mistakes towards Africa, just as Africa made many mistakes for itself as the continent, divided finally into 55 states – but having as many as 2000 historical, cultural and linguistic sub-divisions – learned about statehood as quickly as possible, especially as colonial powers who were weakened by World War II scrambled to get out almost as they, with more avarice, once scrambled to get in; and got out without preparing overmuch apparatus for the government and public administration of the suddenly independent states.

Nigeria had its bloody civil war at the end of the 1960s. Congo fell apart almost from the beginning in the early 1960s. In those countries where the colonial powers refused to get out – as Portugal refuse to decolonise Angola, bloody wars of liberation erupted, fought by competitive liberation movements. In Angola, the Chinese backed the wrong movement. The one supported by the Soviets (and a Cuban army) won. In Zimbabwe, the Chinese backed the right horse and supported Mugabe's armed struggle against white rule. But this meant not only long-lasting friendships – as Zimbabwe has always maintained with China since independence in 1980 – but fast diplomatic footwork to repair relations with those who had won without Chinese help; indeed, had won despite Chinese hinderance as in the case of Angola.

Although, as noted above, China had begun providing developmental assistance to Africa very shortly after Bandung, it is the case that China began a new phase of such assistance – very much tied to future trading partnerships and resource expropriation – only after the liberation era drew to a close; that is, in the 1990s, when South Africa finally attained majority rule under Nelson Mandela and the ANC. It also took China a good ten years after Deng Xiaoping's formal enunciation of the 'four modernisations' in 1978 to get its industrial machine up and running so that it could indeed manufacture commodities for trade and require mineral and petroleum resources of the scale Africa could provide. The removal of political tensions with the US, together with the diplomatic freedoms this allowed, were also important for the Chinese sense of globalisation that, from this period, began to alarm the Western world.

And, having a seat on the UN Security Council – within the concert at last – and realising what this meant, placated all the Chinese conceits about being the 'central kingdom' despite all the years of being marginalised.

Prelude to the new world

Despite the lapsing of the Three World Theory, the aspiration towards a leadership role never fully disappeared in China. As we shall see in a later chapter, this was to be accomplished by economic diplomacy and not political diplomacy. Even so, the enunciation of the theory; together with US diplomatic recognition of China, leading to the UN Security Council seat; and the success of the 'four modernisations' established an era of Chinese prosperity and a peculiar form of Chinese globalisation as its reach began to extend to all corners.

The role of Africa in all of this was pivotal –although it must be stressed that Western alarm about the Chinese purchase of so much economic influence in the continent is born of very demeaning analysis. Firstly, the influence was literally purchased. China did not forcibly colonise Africa as Europe had done. China did not support Apartheid for the sake of mineral expropriation as the US had done. Above all, Africa was not some innocent 'dumb black continent' that could not make choices for itself and for its own advantage. China had often to negotiate hard for its entry-points to Africa. It did so with a new economic model – what might loosely be called the 'Shanghai model', as opposed to a 'Washington model' based on the political imperatives and economic conditionality of the West. The 'Shanghai model' was conditionality-lite, as generous front-loading of liquidity and development projects and funds, preceded Chinese expropriation of mineral and petroleum resources.

If the Africans often drove hard bargains, despite Western fears of African guilelessness and naivety, it must be said that the Chinese themselves often configured Africa in a patronising and superior manner. This was especially true of private Chinese corporations that could be appallingly naïve and racist in their views of how to operate in an African context. For instance appalling Chinese management of Zambian mines led to many deaths of local workers without proper health and safety provisions. This approach extended to a value system that underpinned the official Chinese model.

Even so, the experience and the gains of working in Africa helped the Chinese in their plans for the future. This, as noted above, will be discussed in a later chapter. For now, Africa provided a dawn, a prelude for China.

The Confucian idealism of the Shanghai model

The West has always paraded, alongside its largesse, sometimes as a condition for receiving largesse, values of democracy, plurality and transparency. The Chinese largesse has been depicted as bribery and value-free. In fact, what is probably at work is the Confucian ethic of *guanxi*, very loosely translated as reciprocation. However, this is reciprocation in a chain of vertical hierarchies. Whereas Western values in their purest form are horizontal, as in a democracy, Confucian values are not. Respect and obeisance flow up, as from a subject to an emperor. However, provision and care *must* flow down; otherwise the emperor would lose the mandate of Heaven. Moreover, the higher personage must not only cause value to flow down, he must do so *first*, and, if the recipient below is particularly weak (or underdeveloped) the flow down must be magnificently generous. This says two things: the Chinese view of the African recipient is (perhaps unconsciously) of a weaker and demonstrably less developed entity; the

Chinese frontloading of agreements with copious 'sweeteners' may be seen as part of the Chinese responsibility in a hierarchical arrangement – even when all the rhetoric is about equal partnerships. We have seen how, in the Three World Theory, the underpinning ethos was one of Chinese leadership and, implicitly, superiority.

This sense of leadership was, in a very true sense, an expression of Chinese Realism as an approach to international relations. The country considered it had been powerless. This was a huge psychological shock after millennia of being powerful. Now, it considered it was on the cusp of being powerful again. But, because of its era of humiliation, it had a genuine – if Confucian – sense of solidarity with others who were emerging from the same condition. It was an empathetic idealism mixed with Realism, mixed with the same cultural aloofness that had led China into peril a century before. This time, however, with the world's resources at its command, it was sure it would win.

A meditation

The Chinese case suggests that cultural appreciation becomes important to the understanding of foreign policy – so to the English School's stress on history, and the Copenhagen School's stress on discursive formations, we should add a stress on cultural formations; in the case of China, these would be Confucian; but they would certainly also be, in the English School sense, fully historical, given the intimate memory and recall of the century of humiliation by the imperial powers. The post-World War II US behaviour towards China would have been nothing but a continuing echo of that.

The breakthrough with the US, occasioned largely by Kissinger and Zhou, was intuitive and, insofar as an intuitive actor can be a 'rational' one, was one without the panoply on either side of the apparatus of governmental foreign policy formulation with all its organisational processes, and certainly without its repertoire responses. There simply was no repertoire in this case.

There is a further example of this in Africa, as we shall see in the next chapter, in which Zambian President Kenneth Kaunda entered talks with Apartheid South Africa's F.W. de Klerk in 1989 without any 'rational' preparation, policy briefs, profile briefs on de Klerk at all. For Kaunda, unadvised by either his Ministry of Foreign Affairs or his own State House personnel, it was a 'rationality' formed entirely from intuition and his faith in the moral force of equality and the desire for peace.

In the case of Africa, China set about a lengthy courtship and is receiving, and hopes to receive a lengthy payback as long-term resource agreements come to fruition. Much of this was born of a Chinese empathy for Africa's own humiliation at the hands of the imperial powers, and Zhou Enlai as early as 1956 made almost a fetishistic point about Chinese non-intervention in the affairs of others. This was simultaneously an observation of the foundation tenet of Westphalianism, and also a commitment to Africa that China would not be like the great powers who came to the continent in the 18th and 19th centuries. As we shall see, however, the reformation of the Organisation of African Unity (OAU) into the African Union in 2000 saw the adoption of the principle of non-indifference. It is a principle that has been patchily and selectively, perhaps merely conveniently observed – in the face of the turmoil and slaughters that continue in certain parts of Africa to this day. But the Chinese, wedded to a stance from the mid-20th century, have nothing to say to the formal African stance of the 21st century. Perhaps once again, looking backwards might deny China a chance that comes from looking forward.

Finally, there should be a note about Chinese foreign policy formulation being subjected to the push and pull, in Graham Allison's terms, of different organisations in the official Chinese establishment – all seeking purchase on foreign affairs. There are the organised arms of government, the Ministry of Foreign Affairs itself, and the State Council of the Prime Minister's Cabinet; we can say that the research arms, particularly of the Ministry, have hitherto been weak: there are the foreign policy organs of the People's Liberation Army; and there are, above all, the foreign policy committees of the Chinese Communist Party. Increasingly, as we shall see, Chinese financial institutions command a major say. Of them all, however, the party organs are decisive. And no one knows how they work. In the absence of a figure like Zhou Enlai – and he was properly and purposefully 'inscrutable', as much for the sake of his own political survival as to keep 'his cards close to his chest' – there is no character or personality who may be said to carry a powerful personal ethos into the global realm. To this extent, Kissinger had it easy; his successors today, in seeking to decipher and understand anything, have a rocky ride.

5

African Diplomacy and the Development of Self-Awareness

With the exception of Ethiopia, all of Africa has undergone one form or another of colonialisation – and the Italians had a good go at Ethiopia. The inclusion of Africa in the globalisation of the 18th century involved the European and American slave trade, the outreach of Christian missionaries, trading and resource expropriation projects, and the creation of spheres of influence on the part of individual European powers. This was undertaken differently in North Africa, where there were 'recognisable' state structures of great antiquity, and Sub-Saharan Africa, which was generally viewed as uncivilised, if not savage in its peoples and organisational structures – despite the fact that fully-articulated 'kingship states' existed in many parts of West, East and Southern Africa, and some sent ambassadors to Europe to plead with rulers and the Vatican for a cessation of invasion and slaughter. The Ashante Kingdom in what is now Ghana even traded independently on the futures and commodities markets in London, before that capacity was seized by British colonialism. The palm wine exports to international markets were taken over from the Ashante by British commercial concerns.

At the Berlin Conference of Christmas 1884 to New Year 1885, the European powers agreed to divide Africa formally into colonial territories – doing this according to spheres of influence already achieved, or by the expedient of drawing straight lines on a map. The political cartoons of the day had the negotiators making merry and drinking spirits while carving up both Christmas turkey and a continent. The noteworthy point was that, at that stage, Africa was not considered worth going to war over, and the speed and efficiency of the division was seen as an example of multilateral diplomacy at its successful best. The outcome – today's Africa of 55 independent states which follow closely the boundaries agreed at Berlin – has meant not only a coming to statehood in the impoverished years after World War II, and amidst the turmoil of the Cold War, but coming to statehood with incomplete, divided, or partial nations within the state territory. New 'nations' had to be created to fit the new states, and somehow not repudiate the history of 2000 earlier ethnic and linguistic groups. It has been a diplomatic triumph to make all this work even as well as it has worked till now, and some states, like Zambia, have been huge successes in nationhood despite 72 pre-colonial ethnicities and languages.

The wind of change

Ghana had already become independent in 1957, led by Kwame Nkrumah who, as a student in the US, had been exposed to the ethos of the Harlem Renaissance and the work of Marcus Garvey. He even appropriated Garvey's Black Star emblem for the national flag of Ghana. Most of all, he absorbed the idea of a pan-Africanism, even a pan-blackness. There had been a century of Pan-African Congresses, held in the US and the UK, the Manchester Congress of 1945 being the most important as the nationalist leaders realised that a countdown to independence was one of the results of World War II – the world seeking to make a new start and be rid of the legacy of the old. Those Congresses had included figures such as the black US thinker W.E.B. Dubois, and in 1945 several of the future leaders of Africa. They were a form of Track II or unofficial diplomacy, that all the same was closely linked to what became Track I or official processes and governments. Nigeria and a number of former French colonies gained independence in 1960 and the waves and winds of change seemed unstoppable. Except in Apartheid South Africa.

Insofar as Africa achieved any kind of unity, it was against the racism of the remaining territories in the hands of white minority populations who discriminated against the black majority. The ferocity of that discrimination was certainly enough to galvanise a one-issue unity. Wider unity, despite Nkrumah's inclinations, would take many years longer. But it was not Nkrumah or any other black leader who went to South Africa in 1960 to urge a reconsideration of Apartheid. It was the British Prime Minister, Harold Macmillan. His speech to the South African Parliament was one of those elegant British *tours de force*, understated in tone, careful and precise in wording, but breaking out of obfuscation at just the right moment to be very forceful and direct. Macmillan said a "wind of change" was sweeping the continent.[14] He warned against being swept away. His speech, however, had no effect.

---

[14]   https://www.youtube.com/watch?v=5fjiHI1apUI

Rhodesia

As South Africa, disregarding Macmillan, lurched towards the massacre at Sharpeville and the imprisonment of Nelson Mandela, its neighbours prepared for huge changes. Northern Rhodesia achieved independence as Zambia in 1964. Southern Rhodesia was meant to be next but, in 1965, the white minority government under Ian Smith declared "not in a thousand years" would there be black majority rule[15] – and the minority regime made a Unilateral Declaration of Independence that immediately created an international diplomatic crisis. It became a largely unrecognised government; it was illegal; but it caused huge political problems in the region. Immediately adjacent to Apartheid South Africa, it could serve as a buffer zone for the regime there, and South Africa could make it impossible for international sanctions against Rhodesia to be effective. An impoverished Britain, now led by Prime Minister Harold Wilson, and having to go hand-in-mouth to the IMF for its economic survival, was not going to send in the army. So armed rebellion broke out in Rhodesia, led by two liberation movements. Immediately, the black states in the region had a problem as to which group they should support. And Zambia had a problem, as all its transport routes for its exports and imports ran south through white territory, and its economy could be strangled in a moment. Yet it was staunchly in favour of liberation – while, problematically, President Kaunda was also staunchly a Christian pacifist. Diplomacy became key to Zambia's survival, but it was dangerous diplomacy.

Kaunda hosted one of the two Rhodesian liberation factions (and its army) on Zambian soil, alongside both the exiled African National Congress (ANC) and the South West African people's Organisation (SWAPO) – the two fighting against South Africa, SWAPO for independence in occupied Namibia. But he ordered his own soldiers not to return fire if attacked by marauding Rhodesian or South African commando units, and his air-force not to intercept Rhodesian warplanes flying over Zambian territory. This caused huge resentment within his military, so there was the possibility of domestic problems as well. But he got away with the balancing act, both hosting the antagonists to the white regimes and not directly threatening those regimes himself. Kaunda worked assiduously within the Commonwealth as a multilateral diplomatic organisation, then led by the brilliant Guyanese jurist, Shridath Ramphal.

India, on its own independence in 1947, refused to join anything called a 'British Commonwealth'. The 'Commonwealth of Nations' was thus born, without any British leadership role. In fact, over the Rhodesian issue, the Commonwealth became a primary vehicle for criticising Britain for its inaction.

---

15   https://www.youtube.com/watch?v=FBV3PyvK8Kw

Even so, there was little progress to show for Commonwealth efforts and, in the mid-1970s, it was Henry Kissinger, and then a Anglo-American diplomatic effort led by David Owen and Andrew Young, that sought to find a solution to the Rhodesian problem. There were talks in Geneva. Kaunda himself hosted negotiations on the border between Zambia and Rhodesia (on the Knife Edge Bridge that spanned the two sides of the Victoria Falls, in a railway carriage parked over a line that indicated the border – but no one crossed the line to the other side). Negotiations were leading nowhere, and it took two elements to change the diplomatic stalemate. Robert Mugabe's guerrilla army, operating out of Mozambique, was beginning to tie down the Rhodesian army into a war of attrition. Margaret Thatcher was elected British Prime Minister and declared she wanted to be rid of the Rhodesian albatross, even if it meant recognising a government led by Ian Smith which now, cosmetically, included black faces but was not widely considered to represent a freely-chosen majority rule. A diplomatic furore immediately erupted.

It is well recognised that the 1979 Lusaka Commonwealth summit represented a watershed for the Commonwealth. Leaders came to do battle with Margaret Thatcher over Rhodesia and threatened the demise of the Commonwealth. But it was also a signal moment for African diplomacy. Firstly, there was the role of the summit host, Kenneth Kaunda; secondly, there was the preparatory work Zambian diplomats had put into the occasion, very deliberately to rival and countermand the British preparatory work; and, thirdly, it was an occasion where an African diplomatic effort took place within a fully multilateral, i.e. not only African, environment, with the need to gain allies from far afield, brief interested parties, etc., All these ingredients are needed on such occasions when outcomes are otherwise unpredictable.

There was also the signal role of Commonwealth Secretary-General, Shridath Ramphal, who masterminded many of the tactics at the summit; and the key Zambian diplomat who conducted a pan-African 'shuttle diplomacy' before the summit, garnering support for various options, was Mark Chona. But, put briefly, the occasion was a triumph for diplomacy in an African setting, to say the least – and a triumph for Zambia's role in diplomacy to address an African problem. Peace negotiations were, as a result, convened at Lancaster House in London.

The negotiations at the end of 1979 were tough, but African presidents such as Kaunda, Samora Machel of Mozambique and Julius Nyerere of Tanzania played pivotal behind-the-scenes roles, not only in diplomatic pressure on the British, but pressure also on the liberation parties. Afterwards, in the ensuing military truce and election campaign, African states sent election observers in the world's first coordinated electoral observation – in this case organised by the Commonwealth Secretariat; and Kenyan troops also played a role in the peacekeeping that accompanied the truce. The election of Robert Mugabe, unexpected by the British, satisfied African opinion as his guerrilla army had been perceived as bearing the brunt of the military struggle. It was a victory won by both force of arms and negotiation, and Africa felt it had come of age in the fight against white minority rule. There remained only the huge bastion of South African Apartheid.

Negotiations with the Apartheid government: a meditation on deliberate naivety

Track II, informal and unofficial discussions were held in Lusaka in 1984, as two 'deniable' South African emissaries were sent to form an opinion as to whether substantive negotiations with the ANC were feasible. These were H.W. Van der Merwe, a professor at the University of Cape Town, and Piet Muller, editor of a conservative newspaper. They arrived without any real preparation. In a real way, they were naïve about what to say and how to say it. Even so, as a result, a series of Track II meetings ensued in other parts of Africa in the following years, e.g. involving business leaders in Dakar, but South Africa was also involved in a twin-track process, launching its 'Total Strategy' military onslaught between 1982 and 1984 in an attempt to intimidate all regional governments to the extent that they would neither threaten South Africa themselves, or support liberation movements who did. A principal target was the Marxist government in Angola, host to a Cuban army that had, in the final battles for independence from Portugal in 1975-6, fought an earlier South African incursion to a standstill. Borrowed from the French attempt to suppress the Algerian uprising, South African Total Strategy ruined large parts of the region. The Zimbabweans, whose air-force had been destroyed by South African saboteurs in 1982, fought against a South African proxy guerrilla force in Mozambique but it was really as late as 1988, with the mass battle lines and clashes around the Angolan city of Cuito Cuanavale, that the Cuban forces – aided by the Soviet air-force – finally forced South Africa to a proper negotiating table. 1986 Commonwealth efforts by the Commonwealth Secretary-General, now the Nigerian Emeka Anyaoku, and a Commonwealth Eminent Persons Group co-chaired by former Nigerian President Olusegun Obasanjo, were unsuccessful – even with the threat of sanctions in tow. The post 1988 talks were led by the US diplomat, Chester Crocker. These were talks of South African military disengagement and withdrawal from non-South African territories – such as Namibia – but they did not concern a peace in the region that would emanate from majority rule.

Even so, the upheaval in the ranks of the Apartheid government was immense. President Botha was forced to resign. In his place was appointed the largely unknown F.W. de Klerk and, in 1989, he sent private messages to President Kaunda, asking for peace talks. In the same year, talks were also proceeding with Thabo Mbeki in the south of England. These were secret, but the talks with Kaunda were milked by Zambian and international media. De Klerk needed Kaunda to leverage Mbeki's ANC, but also to secure a buy-in to any peace deal from the 'frontline' states of the region that had both confronted South Africa and been militarily destabilised by it.

De Klerk, reputedly, entered these talks at Livingstone by the Victoria Falls, with five ring-binders of comprehensive notes on President Kaunda. By contrast, Kaunda went in without any briefing whatsoever. Both his Ministry of Foreign Affairs and staff at State House had not expected the rise of de Klerk, and neither had any information on de Klerk. Kaunda didn't ask for any either. So, as intimated at the end of the preceding chapter, he went in entirely trusting on his intuition, his moral position on behalf of peace and equality – and against the advice of his colleague presidents such as Tanzania's Julius Nyerere; they certainly had no trust in the South Africans, and could point to a long list of bad faith on the part of the Apartheid regime, i.e. there were rational reasons not to negotiate. For Kaunda, rationality evolved during the talks themselves, and this might be just as well as, essentially, his starting point was not only one of openness but deliberate naivety. Mandela was released early the next year, and the ANC unbanned in South Africa. How much this was due to Kaunda, how much to Mbeki, and whether any of this could have happened without Cuban victory at Cuito Cuanavale, can be debated. The three probably went together. Although it should be said that Mbeki, having spent most of his adult life outside South Africa, could not fully maintain a stance that he was negotiating for South Africans. He and Kaunda were negotiating for a place for the ANC in a democratised South Africa; and Mbeki had the leverage of insurrection and rebellion. The release of Mandela, the completion of the anti-colonial and anti-minority-rule project allowed African diplomacy to begin its coming of age.

African Union and Nigerian diplomacy

The Commonwealth's role in international affairs as an organisation with a large membership but then still largely informalised modes of diplomatic intervention allowed both Ramphal and Anyaoku as Secretaries-General to act as scaled-down variants of the UN Secretary-General as epitomised by Dag Hammarskjold. Those who followed Hammarskjold never emulated his daring and diplomatic risk-taking, but it could be said that Ramphal (over the independence of Zimbabwe) and Anyaoku (over pressure on South Africa) did – in both cases confronting UK Prime Minister Margaret Thatcher. It could also be argued that Kofi Annan, of Ghanaian origin, sought to be a quiet and subtle form of Hammarskjold and overcome the legacy of his immediate predecessors as UN Secretary-General who were loathe to be daring. It meant the advent of African-derived diplomatic leaderships in wider arenas than just Southern Africa.

Much of this had to concern peacekeeping and its allied diplomacy. Since 1960 there have been 18 fully-fledged civil wars, and 11 what have been called genocides. In the decade of the 1980s, there were over 3 million fatalities of such violence. At the beginning of the 1990s, 43% of the world's refugee population was within Africa.

Annan had not been successful or even urgent as Deputy Secretary-General over the early stages of the genocide in Rwanda, but that event was probably key in persuading the African Union, reborn from the Organisation of African Unity in 1999, to adopt a policy of non-indifference to regional conflicts. Before, the OAU had been unsuccessful in peacekeeping and peacemaking. Its 1977-82 efforts in Chad were its greatest foray into the realm of coordinated action, but was handicapped by logistical shortcomings and mobilisation problems. The OAU undertook its mission because it received permission from the government in Chad. Hitherto, the doctrine of non-intervention, drawn from the foundation principles of the Non-Aligned Movement, which drew in turn from Zhou Enlai's 1955 Bandung speech, had prevented any unilateral peacekeeping, or even forceful diplomacy backed up by militarised preparation. The need to be invited into a state-in-conflict, rather than being able to intervene in an atrocious conflict on the grounds of human rights and humanitarian concerns; or on grounds of instability threatening surrounding states; was a huge question mark about the capacity and limits of OAU diplomacy. Even in Chad, although OAU mediation began in 1977, it took until 1981 before peacekeeping soldiers arrived, and they were never able to deploy in a sustained and supported way. Even in this case, the OAU followed a Nigerian initiative, accepted the Chadian government's formal position that it was at war with Libya, through Libyan proxies, and was not actually undergoing civil war. OAU peacekeeping forces of 1981 followed upon an earlier deployment of Nigerian soldiers in 1979. It marked Nigeria as having a diplomatic interest in the west and centre of Africa.

This was chiefly illustrated by other efforts at peacekeeping/making such as that which occurred from 1990 to 1997 in Sierra Leone and Liberia. This was undertaken by the regional African Grouping, using armed forces under the ECOMOG (ECOWAS Monitoring Group) banner, led mainly by Nigerian troops acting on behalf of ECOWAS (Economic Community of West African States), that blasted its way in to a temporary form of peace in both Liberia and Sierra Leone – but which did not end violence and war in the region, especially in Liberia.

What it did was to cement Nigerian peacekeeping/making diplomacy as capable of militarised initiatives. Even so, Nigerian President Olusegun Obasanjo relied on non-military diplomatic means, when Chairman of the African Union, 2004-6, on the issue of Darfur. The slaughters in that Sudanese province had horrified the world. Obasanjo hosted several summits of interested parties in his capital, Abuja. He had local reason to do so, as neighbouring Chad was beginning to host nearly a quarter of a million refugees from the Darfur conflict. But, by this time, the old OAU doctrine of non-intervention had given way to the new AU doctrine of non-indifference. Even so, although the AU in 2004 recognised that 'the humanitarian situation in Darfur is serious', it would not unilaterally intervene. In 2007, it did so in association with the UN, and the military side of peacekeeping depended on hybrid forces, involving not only African troops under AU colours but those from Europe and elsewhere under UN colours; but also involving the logistical means and equipment brought by those UN forces. The intervention required UN Security Council Resolution 1769, and this was an escalation from UN Security Council Resolution 1564, which was an ultimatum to the Sudanese government to accept AU peacekeepers in Darfur under the rubric of the AU Mission to Sudan (AMIS) – and these peacekeepers were first led by Rwandan and Nigerian soldiers. But what it meant was that, once again, the AU like the OAU before it was unable or unwilling to intervene unilaterally in a matter of grave humanitarian and diplomatic concern.

Subsequent AU efforts in Darfur to find a lasting diplomatic solution have been led by former South African President Thabo Mbeki (2009-14) and Mbeki sought to instigate a version of the power-sharing formula he had pioneered in both Democratic Republic of Congo (2002) and, contentiously, in Zimbabwe (2007-8) – but these have been unsuccessful. President Jacob Zuma of South Africa briefly attempted the same inclusiveness peace formula in the Libyan crisis in 2011, again under AU colours.

Norms such as the 'responsibility to protect' have had a hard time gaining unanimous adherence within the AU. Slowly, however, the norm is gaining traction and this owes somewhat to deliberations within the AU's Peace and Security Council (established 2004), which has the African Standby Force as an associated programme. In fact the Standby Force is a series of regional such forces, and it was the Southern African Development Community (SADC) military initiative, involving South African and Tanzanian troops that engaged the Congolese M23 rebels - the most notorious of the many violent rebel groups in Democratic Republic of Congo - in 2013. Their success, under both SADC and UN Security Council resolutions, was treated as a military victory, but owed greatly to sustained diplomatic pressure on Rwanda's President Kagame from the UN.

Annan in Kenya and Mbeki in Zimbabwe – and a mediation on values and democracy as mediated by diplomacy

What Mbeki tried to do in Darfur echoed his controversial mediation in the aftermath of the extremely controversial Zimbabwean elections of 2008. This in turn was reminiscent of Annan's mediation in the equally controversial elections aftermath in Kenya in 2007. Both men were the representatives of African multilateral diplomacy: Annan of the AU, and Mbeki of SADC. Both came up with similar 'solutions' – more like 'settlements' than solutions, but true solutions may well have been impossible in both cases. Annan took considerably less time, and left sanction and sting in the tail of his mediation, namely International Criminal Court (ICC) indictments of those involved in orchestrating electoral violence (although these cases before the ICC have largely failed).

But both mediations resulted in the continuation of Presidencies that had been in place before the elections, even though, in both elections, the opposition leader probably won, and should have been appointed President. Violence and rigging produced what were in all probability falsified results. Even so, in both cases, the rightfully 'victorious' opposition leader did not become President – but became instead a specially created Prime Minister, an office below that of the President and which did not previously constitutionally exist.

Where electoral results were honoured was in a proportional representation, not in the European Parliamentary sense, but in the sense of numbers of seats in the Cabinet. The party with most votes had the most Cabinet seats. Neither main party was excluded from these spoils of office.

Mbeki in particular would have said that the outcome represented, in the Cabinet allocations, the spirit of democracy, and this – together with having both major political leaders in one administration as President and Prime Minister – represented an 'African' value of inclusiveness. It was an inclusiveness engineered in such a way that violence was removed from the power struggle, and with this removal came the end of slaughter. So that, as well as inclusiveness, the universal value of human lives was promoted.

It is a controversial formula. In neither country was this formula repeated in the elections that followed five years later. But the formula did ensure a discernible species of peace and, through peace, stability in each case for five years. Mbeki would say, and Annan would not disagree, that their 'African diplomacy' had purchased an 'African solution' that, all the same, championed the most basic of universal values.

What this means is an African diplomacy, that has not only come of age, but brings something new – controversially so – that is perhaps of benefit to the continent, and possibly to the contemplation of just electoral outcomes in the wider world.

6

The Imponderables of Middle Eastern Diplomacy: An Historical Catalogue of Disasters and Deferments

Apart from the *rapprochement* with China, Henry Kissinger would probably best view his record with Egypt and Israel in mind – helping to consolidate the post-1973 'peace' between the two, and setting into motion the US policy of copious foreign aid, with huge military resources as a key feature, so that neither state could maintain their security apparatus and ambitions without the US. This crafted a dependency, but also a balance of power between Israel and Egypt – one in which Israel always had a slightly greater arsenal – but the tilt in the balance was never enough to tip the scales. It reflected the typical Kissinger-esque love of the concert as a means of executing international relations; only this Middle Eastern concert could not be played without constant reference to the US. It might have consolidated the peace between two states; it did nothing to solve the vexatious problems of the region, especially that between the Israelis and the Palestinians.

There is some irony in that Kissinger's latest (and probably last) book, *World Order*, sub-titled *Reflections on the Character of Nations and the Course of History*, reveals that he has learned little from the disastrous history of the Middle East since his time in office. The book is essentially a root and branch defence of the Westphalian state. Where it is a somewhat radical book is its open questioning of whether Saudi Arabia is a true Westphalian state, or an Islamic one with a huge range of problems emanating from it into international relations. Kissinger is fearful of an Islamic state system. But, in the same book, he holds up Israel as a properly Westphalian state. It has been nothing of the sort – both expanding its boundaries unilaterally, defying international law and UN resolutions, reneging on agreements, occupying the territory of other states, and refusing to allow statehood to the Palestinians - choosing to occupy and exploit large chunks of Palestinian territory, which Israel had itself agreed to be Palestinian, as if Palestine were the colony of a militarised colonial overlord.

The messy environment for foreign policy and diplomacy

The Arab-Israeli wars

The Balfour Declaration of 1917 proposed the partition of Palestine into two states and one was to be Jewish. This was meant to satisfy the Zionist movement seeking a 'homeland for the Jews'. Early Zionism did not necessarily see this homeland as being located in the Middle East, let alone in the historical area of Biblical Israel. Locations in Africa and South America entered the list of possibilities. But the sense of needing to do something definitive and swiftly for the Jews became an urgency in the wake of World War II, especially in the light of the gigantic atrocities and attempted genocide of the Holocaust. The international community agreed, and the British mandate over Palestine that had begun after World War I, carved out of the defeated Ottoman Empire, was to become a United Nations mandate for the final step towards a new state. There was much confusion during the transition from the British to the UN, and the Palestinian population certainly resisted the process with its *Nakba* or liberation war named after the 'day of catastrophe' when a huge part of the Palestinian population fled the encroaching Jews. Jewish terrorist movements used violent insurrection to force the pace of independence and, finally, in 1948, Ben Gurion was able to declare the birth of Israel. Almost immediately, the armies of the surrounding Arab states launched a multi-front attack on Israel. This was partly in solidarity with the Palestinians, but also very much to resist what would have been a changed political situation in their region and a great complication to their existing regional balance of power. It would also make part of the Middle East no longer Arabic and no longer Islamic – although, in 1948, the Arabic factor was greater than any Islamic factor. There was a slow motion movement towards modernity – expressed a little later in the seizure of power in Egypt by Nasser and the Free Officers – and the public desire for a new and unified Arabia. Israel was an intrusion upon all these dreams.

The Arab armies were antiquated and very poorly generaled. Nasser himself, as a young officer, became almost legendary simply for refusing to surrender. The Israeli forces were totally victorious and, in the place of the victim who went passively to the gas chambers, the image and the legend of the 'fighting Jew' was born – and has never changed. The ill-advised assault of the Suez Canal zone in 1956, alongside British and French contingents, to ensure

Nasser could not nationalise the canal – which was on Egyptian soil – ended in retreat because of strong diplomatic pressure from the US and UN but, once again, when the Israeli and Egyptian forces engaged, the Egyptians lost. With Soviet help, Nasser in response began building a new army with the latest equipment. The tanks looked splendid on the parade ground and the warplanes looked splendid parked in formation on their runways.

They were almost literally in such positions when the Israelis decimated the Egyptian forces and those of Syria in 1967. Much has been made of the precursor manoeuvres of Nasser, in demanding the withdrawal of the UN peacekeeping forces inserted into the Sinai Peninsula as part of the disengagement after 1956. They were meant to act as a buffer force between the Egyptians and the Israelis. Nasser, in 1967, not only demanded they leave but set up his newly equipped army in a display of force facing the Israelis. A recent school of thought suggests that Nasser was setting about a gigantic bluff; he had asked only for the repositioning of the UN force; and his chief concern was that the Israelis were preparing an attack on Syria, which at that time was politically very close to Egypt and there was even popular demand for a unified Egyptian/Syrian State, a United Arab Republic; so Nasser's military display was calibrated to make the Israelis think twice about an attack on Syria, as there would be an Egyptian threat to their rear. In the event, the Israelis called the bluff and simply attacked both – brilliantly and pre-emptively – destroying the Egyptian air-force, meticulously lined up on the runways, and cutting a swathe through the Egyptian tanks that certainly looked intimidating as a display, but which were not in proper battle order. They took all of Sinai right up to the bank of the Suez Canal. On the Syrian front, they took the Golan Heights. Ironically, against the Egyptians the Israelis used German Panzer tactics, pioneered by Guderian in the attack on France, where there was no central focus of their attack. Instead of one spearhead there were multiple arrowheads with tank battalion commanders given huge discretion. Egyptian military doctrine could not have responded in any case.

It was Nasser's successor, Sadat, who was determined in 1973 to recapture the Sinai Peninsula from the Israelis. At the time of Yom Kippur, a Jewish festival, Egyptian troops stormed across the Canal. Pre-empting the Israeli tank tactics of 1967, Sadat's frontline forces were arrayed in small independent units armed with surface-to-surface anti-tank missiles. With no fixed, centrally-directed command, their locations were unpredictable and, as the tanks came forward, nests of Egyptian anti-tank commandos unleashed their missiles. The first stages of the conflict were a huge victory for the Egyptians. The Israeli counter-attack might have succeeded in nullifying this, but emergency diplomacy involving the superpowers, with Kissinger to the fore, imposed a ceasefire. All the same, for the Egyptians it was a huge restoration of morale and self-belief. They regained the Sinai, although it took further diplomacy by Kissinger to complete the process, and there was never another war between Egypt and Israel. The Syrians, however, were never to regain the Golan Heights. Their advancing tanks were halted by concentrated Israeli airstrikes, although for a considerable period the battles waxed and waned, and it must be said there was huge valour and military thought on both sides. Afterwards, both sides used proxies to harass the other, but there was never another war between Israel and Syria.

The Israeli invasions of Lebanon

From 1975 Israel helped organise and support an allied militia, a Maronite Christian militia, led by Major Haddad, in the south of Lebanon. It was to act as a check to Syrian ambitions for influence in Lebanon but also, more particularly, to establish a buffer zone between Israel and Palestinian forces who, after their ouster from Jordan in the so-called 'Black September' pogroms of 1970-1, had headquartered themselves under the Palestine Liberation Organisation (PLO) umbrella in Lebanon. Jordan had expelled the PLO because of fears that the Palestinian population on Jordanian territory was growing so swiftly there would be a temptation for the PLO simply to seize the Jordanian state and make it their own. Many Israeli strategists were encouraging of this possibility. It would have solved the problem of the Palestinians not having a state, and the 1967 Israeli seizure of the West Bank, up till then the envisaged Palestinian 'homeland', had not been reversed by the Egyptian successes of 1973; so the prospect was that Israel could keep the West Bank with fewer problems if the Palestinians took Jordan. The Jordanian expulsion of the PLO only saw it grow in strength in Lebanon and it became a critical force in Lebanese politics. The harassing and buffer capacities of Haddad's militia aside, it was only a matter of time before the Israelis invaded Lebanon.

They did this in 1978, but were curiously unsuccessful in that the Palestinian forces occupying southern Lebanon were able to withdraw almost completely intact. It created, however, a huge Palestinian refugee crisis as the Israelis left Haddad to police the areas they had seized and the Palestinian population fled towards Beirut. The growth of Palestinian refugee camps around Beirut would provide sites of slaughter in the Israeli invasion of 1982. This time, the assault was on Beirut itself – the Paris of the eastern Mediterranean, capital city of a most uneasy but somewhat managed polity of Islamic and Christian mixtures, and major city of a land that, in the reputed days of King Solomon, willingly and generously provided beams of cedar to build the Israeli temple in Jerusalem.

The PLO put out a call for international brigades to come to its assistance and prepared to dig in for an urban war that would have destroyed the beautiful city. Clashes did begin, but a huge international diplomatic effort ensured that the Palestinian forces could leave brandishing their weapons and claiming at least a moral victory – they had not in fact been militarily defeated – but they had to find a new exile home in Tunis. The Israelis were happy, in that Tunis was at the other end of the Mediterranean and the PLO grip on the region would not be as strong. But the PLO withdrawal left the Palestinian refugee camps without protection, and Haddad's militia killed in cold blood the inhabitants of Sabra and Shatila; some estimates point to 3,500 fatalities; mostly Palestinians and a number of Lebanese Shi'a Muslims. The Shi'a element would return to haunt the Israelis.

So that the final Israeli assault on Lebanon was precisely to root out the Shi'a militia and political group, Hezbollah – that in fact held many seats in the Lebanese Parliament, and so were a *bona fide* force in Lebanese politics, as well as being a disruptive one through its militia and through its alliances with Syria and Iran – the latter being the Shi'a stronghold of the world. But the Hezbollah forces stood and fought the Israelis, firstly bunkered down and dug underground as the tank columns passed, then bursting into the open to attack from within the Israeli formations. The Israelis had not expected the toughness of the resistance, and had underestimated the Iranian training of Hezbollah. By this time, Israeli military doctrine was no longer as daring as during the 1967 war, and in any case the terrain of Lebanon did not lend itself to that kind of multi-arrow-head attack. The doctrine was almost conventional, and the Hezbollah militia had no trouble reading it. But, as the Israelis pulled back, they realised the enemy of the future would be Iran; and the new Iranian President Ahmedinejad, elected in 2005, was not averse to sabre-rattling and certainly not shy to alert the world to an Iranian nuclear development programme.

In 2006 as well, in the Palestinian legislative elections, Fatah, the dominant political party of the PLO, having failed to deliver anything like a real independence because of the success of Israeli policies – and having grown immensely corrupt as well as inefficient – were defeated by Hamas who took 74 of the 132 seats. And Hamas was supported by Syria and Iran. But how had Fatah and the PLO returned from its exile in Tunis to become the government of what was called the Palestinian Authority? We turn now from wars to the almost as vexed diplomacy deployed upon the region. This involved the US at Presidential level – but it was the Egyptian President Sadat who, with immense daring, first sought a sudden irreversible breakthrough.

A meditation: the pharaoh goes to David's city

In the divisive scriptures and legends of the region, the Jewish people have in fact an intimate relationship with the Lebanese, the Iranians and the Egyptians – the Lebanese, as mentioned above, because of King Hiram's despatching the cedars of Lebanon to Solomon to build the temple; the Iranians, or Persians as they then were, for the release of the Jewish people from Babylonian captivity with permission to rebuild that temple; and the Egyptians who enslaved them but, before then, had appointed Joseph, under the Pharaoh, as prime minister of Egypt. Many years later came David, who established the seat of the fledging kingdom of Israel, as it emerged from a mere federation of tribes, in Jerusalem.

In 1977, four years after the Egyptian recapture of Sinai, President Sadat went to Jerusalem. The Israelis had only a few days' notice that he wanted to come and were in consternation at this wholly unexpected and unpredicted development. They realised they had to agree or be seen as the side that had refused an opportunity for peace. Sadat had shared his decision with a close group of advisers, not all of whom agreed with the initiative but, insofar as the President seemed determined to go ahead, this was a 'rational actor' moment – although, like Kaunda's with de Klerk in Southern Africa, impulsive and trusting on intuition. The difference was that the Egyptians had no end of briefing materials on Israel and its leadership. Sadat took on board this material, but still seemed to trust intuitively to a moral breakthrough. Having said that, he, having waged war on Israel, would have known from previous briefings the perils and balances of gains and losses he was now about to encounter – so that the organisational processes and politics of the past would not have been fully absent. However, he certainly did not act according to a repertoire. His action was entirely new, original and daring.

In the wake of his visit, his amazing and morally-pitched rhetoric to the Israeli Knesset, and the international press coverage it received – almost all glowing and, indeed, hopeful – it seemed both that some sort of peace might be possible, and that the Egyptians had seized the moral high ground.[16] For Sadat, having both claimed a military triumph (although, as noted above, had the 1973 conflict continued, that might not have been the case) and a diplomatic/moral one, he would have felt in a secure position. President Jimmy Carter hosted both Sadat and Israeli Prime Minister Begin at Camp David in 1978, and the famous 'walk in the woods', with Carter conducting personalised diplomacy while wearing a jumper, did indeed seem to establish a formal peace between Egypt and Israel. This was less three 'rational actors' working together in a spontaneous fashion and in an informalised situation.

---

[16]   https://www.youtube.com/watch?v=aetcAAWc8DA

Each would have been very carefully briefed and rehearsed – again not in any repertoire sense, since peace had not been achieved between them before, but in the cut and thrust of concessions and conditions. The fact that, in the end, it was reasonably straight-forward did not mean there had been no such preparations.

And there was one looming caveat: this was a peace between Egypt and Israel. The Palestinians had not been invited to Camp David. Sadat did not speak for them. He did not speak for the Arab world. He spoke for Egypt. And he certainly did not speak for what was then regarded as an unimportant fringe player in the Palestinian equation, Iran. The Iranian Revolution took place in 1979, and suddenly what seemed like a militant, unpredictable, to some irrational, Shi'a presence burst upon the scene with international as well as Middle Eastern consequences. The US was certainly dismayed and encouraged Saddam Hussein's Iraq to wage war against Iran from 1980-4, with huge financing channelled through Saudi Arabia. Saddam did not win this war but, suddenly, he was more powerful too.

The Palestinians, chagrined over their exclusion from Camp David, mindful that the PLO leadership had been marginalised within Palestine by exile in distant Tunis, and seeing no diplomatic or negotiating progress on the ground, rose up in the first *Intifada* of 1987-91. And 1991 was also the year, when emboldened by US support in his war with Iran, Saddam made the fateful mistake of invading Kuwait and setting into train the First Gulf War. The region was in flames. Even Syria sent troops to fight alongside the US and its coalition. Everyone forgot about the Palestinians. The 'new world order' that emerged, seemingly as a consolidation of the fall of communism in 1989, had no place for a people seemingly condemned to live on the fringes of diplomacy and nationhood.

A further meditation: Oslo, for better or worse

We have seen how, in 1984 in Lusaka, Track II diplomacy was utilised by Track I actors to test possible avenues for future Track I or official, governmental negotiations. In starkest terms, Track I refers to official state or recognised international agency diplomacy; and Track II are unofficial actors. It is rare for a Track II initiative to be able to claim a major diplomatic success without first reference to a future tie-in with Track I. An exception may be in the process that led to the Oslo Accords, beginning in 1993 – when a group of academics pondered a peace plan that would include the Palestinians and satisfy both them and the Israelis. They entered where 'angels' such as Sadat and Carter had feared to tread. Amazingly, their outline plan was bold but realistic enough to garner almost immediate Track I admiration and adoption

– or perhaps 'adaptation' might be the better term as Oslo 2 began to put detailing into place, and these talks in the second stage of the Oslo process were commanded by Track I negotiators, although this had not been envisaged or pre-arranged in the first instance.

It was Oslo 2 that in 1995 set into place a stage-by-stage plan for Palestinian statehood – a Palestinian Administrative Authority being established at the first stage. Yasser Arafat and the PLO, marginalised in Tunis, were desperate to be integrated into the process, and to become the Administrative Authority. But they took to the talks a skeleton delegation, in which only one person was a lawyer who spoke English and who could understand the detailing of the final Accords. Even so, the problem of the final Accords was not so much in their wording – although a system of guarantees might certainly have helped – but their later implementation. The most controversial and difficult part of the Accords was the division of the land into Categories A, B, and C. Category C land was controlled by the Israelis, but would eventually become Category B. Category B land was jointly controlled by the Israelis and Palestinians, but would eventually become Category A. Category A land, the minority portion around the major Palestinian cities, would be from the outset under Palestinian Authority control. A fully-fledged Palestinian state would emerge as the land passed fully into Palestinian hands. But it never really happened. Israeli settlements began to dominate huge portions of Category C and large parts of Category B land. Category A land was not immune to Israeli interventions. Israel controlled the majority of the water resources, without which land could not be fully farmed. And Israel closed down the only Palestinian airport, so that access to 'Palestine' involved first entry and scrutiny in Israel; or entry via Jordan, with its own troubled Palestinian history. And Gaza was a geographically separate enclave – although Prime Minister Sharon did withdraw Israeli settlements from Gaza. They have, however, proliferated on the West Bank.

The slow motion to non-existent progress of land transfer, and the countermanding growth of settlements led the new Palestinian Authority into a huge credibility deficit with its own people. Arafat himself compounded the problems by not making the transition from guerrilla leader to a prime ministerial figure. Palestinian public administration was chaotic and awful, and became corrupt and patron-driven. But the major issue was land. It seemed the Oslo Accords were doomed in their promise. And the Israelis had worked out that it was better to have the PLO not in distant Tunis, but pleading with them close to hand in a dependent relationship. President Clinton convened Arafat and Israeli Prime Minister Barak at Camp David in 2000, in a doomed effort to salvage the Oslo Accords – but to no real effect. The second *Intifada* broke out in 2000 and went on to 2005. Unlike the first *Intifada*, which had a genuine spontaneity, the second was urged on by the PLO as its violent symbol of resistance to Israeli bad faith. It did not change Israeli policy and, in 2005, President Ahmedinejad took office in Iran, with both his nuclear development policy and his clear antipathy towards Israeli Zionism. In 2006, with support from Iran, Hamas won a huge victory in the Palestinian elections, and civil war broke out in Palestine between Hamas and a PLO reluctant to surrender power – and supported by a US who was far from rigorous in its demands for an observation of democratic outcomes. Hamas was driven from the West Bank, but retained control of Gaza. This was followed by three wars between Gaza and Israel.

Before we look at the return to war, it might be worthwhile to make two observations: the first is a simple one, and that is the difficulty Track II has in laying conditions or demanding guarantees for the Track I take up of its accomplishments; once Track I takes up, or takes over, the negotiating process, it is up to official representatives within an official process to negotiate professionally and properly. This leads to the second observation: the PLO did not negotiate well in Oslo 2. It had neither experience nor expertise in sufficient amounts for what became a seemingly amazing breakthrough that was, all the same, fraught with risks. A gigantic leap of faith would have been required under any circumstances, but an under-negotiated leap was totally perilous. Arafat and his delegation had no history of research, no history or culture of organisational processes and the scrutiny that comes from what competitive agencies and ministries apply to one another. Arafat as 'rational actor' was perhaps driven by a lifelong moral and national quest, but it seems he was also driven by desperation – and that is the least desirable element in any species of 'rationality'.

Gaza, Egypt and Israel

Greatly complicating the picture was recent history: the attacks of 9/11 occurred in 2001. Gulf War II broke out in 2003, as the Western armies marched into Iraq. As a result of the second *Intifada*, a 'quartet' involving the US, the UN, the EU and Russia was established in 2002; it was intended to act as some kind of diplomatic 'shotgun' in the Israeli/Palestinian situation – but it was missing key actors. Iran might beneficially have been one. And Egypt, who under Sadat had become an icon of peace with Israel, now had a joint interest with Israel in the containment of Hamas in Gaza. The Egyptian concern with Hamas was the relationship between Hamas and the Muslim Brotherhood, banned in Egypt, and the only significantly organised opposition to the descendants of Nasser and Sadat who, as military men wearing suits, ruled the country with a growing lack of imagination and a growing sense of self-interest. It is no accident that the Arab Spring had its greatest popular manifestation on the streets and squares of Cairo. But it meant, for Gaza, an imprisonment with Israeli checkpoints on one side, and Egyptian checkpoints on the other, and an Israeli maritime blockade at sea. Militant Gazans took to firing homemade rockets at Israel. They, for the most part, caused little damage – but did invite massive Israeli retaliation. The assaults of 2008-9, 2012, and 2014 caused increasing amounts of damage; that of 2014 left a trail of huge destruction and ruination of a city that has become perhaps the largest concentration camp or, speaking less dramatically, largest ghetto – in the old European sense of Jewish ghettos – on earth. No solution, or even settlement of the problems in this part of the world will ever become possible unless not only Israel and Palestine conclude successful negotiations, but Palestinian factions achieve successful negotiations between themselves, and Israel and Egypt both agree a joint outcome; and Iran is satisfied that its ally, Hamas, is justly served. As for being justly or fairly served, there has been no election in Palestine since 2006. And, even if all these participating parties find themselves amenable to one another, there is still of course the vexed question of land. Even if all the settlements were withdrawn, or even if Palestine agreed to all the settlements remaining with, for instance, autonomous municipal rights, where exactly would Israel end and Palestine start? What would the borders be?

Borders as an expanding phenomenon

Unlike almost every other conflict, where borders have been inscribed in earlier agreements or treaties, those between Israel and Palestine have changed dramatically over the years – and each change has signalled a shrinkage of Palestine.

The original borders, those under the UN Mandate that were meant to demarcate the territorial limits of Israel, were precisely the borders at independence in 1948. However, the defeat of the invading Arab armies in 1949 meant a huge increase in the size of Israel as military forces occupied land seized from the defeated neighbours. The new borders were in fact recognised internationally as the 'Green Lines'. However, the war of 1967 meant the forward pushing of borders yet again and, although not all of these were sustained (Egypt retook the Sinai in 1973; the West Bank of Jordan became the Palestinian 'future state', albeit with a large number of Jewish settlements and Israeli control of much land; but Israel annexed the Golan from Syria), it meant an increase in size even so. The Geneva Accord lines of 2003 tried to recognise *fait accompli* and these represent the furthest extent of formal international acceptance of an enlarged Israel – but do not include the settlements and do not recognise the further intrusion into Palestinian territory of the Israeli wall. It would seem that, even should the settlements issue be resolved, the wall would represent the only acceptable border for the

Israeli state. Palestine would become a small emirate or, if the settlements remain as formal extensions of Israel, a necklace of separated 'free Palestinian cities' with very little agricultural hinterland or assured contiguity. In the light of the original Balfour Declaration, which proposed (certainly by comparison with the reality today) a sort of equitable partition, we would have very little we could call a Palestinian state. The problems for future diplomacy seem intractable.

7

Insider and Outsider: Israel's Demons in the New Millennium

As Israel consolidated its place in the Middle East, few anymore questioned its right to exist – but many questioned its right to exist within its expansionist borders; questioned also its treatment of those within its borders who were destined for all foreseeable future to be denied citizenship rights, that is the Palestinians living within Israel; and of course questioned the colonisation by settlers, patch by patch, of Palestinian land. But, insofar as those borders enclosed Palestinian populations – populations that expanded both by natural birth rate and by expulsion from Palestinian territory – the Israelis began to feel an internal dilemma that mirrored the dilemmas and threats they perceived externally. It led to a discourse of insecurity, the need for securitisation, and the sense of an existential threat to the nature of the Jewish person with a Jewish identity within the Jewish homeland that was the essence of the Jewish state. What if Palestinians came to outnumber, within the borders of Israel, the Jews? And what if, by sheer weight of numbers and cultural practice, including religious practice, the Jewish identity based on a Jewish culture began to change?

The analysis of the Jewish scholar, Uriel Abulof, superbly rendered, of the discourse of 'deep securitisation' over in particular Israel's 'demographic demon', i.e. the size of the Palestinian population within Israel overtaking the size of the Jewish population, and how this is a genuine 'existential threat', is an example of excellent scholarship that blends theory with analysis. The theory of which he speaks essentially derives from the Copenhagen School of International Relations – which added to the English School's concern for historical context an emphasis on discursive formations. There is a complication of course in the neatness of the theory's approach: if the state may be discursively 'constructed' in Foucauldian terms, how does the state in turn play any determining role in constructing its citizens? What is the nature of the feedback loop? What are the characteristics of a virtuous circle when all manner of disruptions and jagged edges in fact interrupt this circle? In one article, these questions are not Abulof's concern. What is his concern is a step-by-step analysis of Israeli discourse to do with the threat of Palestinian demographics. He is able to depict this as a very real threat, and one serious enough to be regarded as an existential threat: identity, the practice of identity, the security and assuredness of identity are imperilled. The importance of this was within living memory, in a land which declared its purpose was to retrieve Jewish identity from the butchery of the Holocaust and preceding centuries of European marginalisation – and this declaration, the formation of this state which was to do this, to do this within a homeland for the Jews where Jews and their identity would be secure at last, even if they had to fight for it. Within one lifetime, it had been threatened from without, and now it was threatened from within.

Hostility towards the Palestinian population and the idea of a Palestinian state perhaps derives from, among other things, a distaste of doing something to accommodate a threat. But, while it has led to all manner of confusion and belligerence in domestic policy and policy towards Palestine both as a concept and as an Administrative Authority, it adds to a sense that everything is a threat – and, if the 'traditional' enemies of Egypt and Jordan are now placated, and Syria has other concerns on its mind, and the Arab League in general, despite rhetoric, is hardly pushing the Palestinian issue or indeed any issue that might threaten Israel, the need for an enemy nearby, even if not immediately neighbouring, is fulfilled by Iran.

The Persia that birthed Israel and Christianity

The ironies that emerge from the region's history are immense. We have noted King Hiram's provision of the Cedars of Lebanon for King Solomon's temple. This is from the Biblical account and we have no other evidence either existed. We do have evidence for the Persian political ethics that allowed the Jews, held in Babylonian captivity, to return to Jerusalem to rebuild their temple – which was completed about 516 BC. This evidence is in the form of the Cyrus Cylinder (held in the British Museum) from 539-8 BC, which has been described as the world's first charter of human rights – but which is King Cyrus's promulgation of religious freedom; and it was probably under its rubric that the Jews were able to rebuild the temple and worship freely. Certainly, the Biblical book of Esther tells of how the Persian King Ahasuerus (probably Xerxes I, 518-465 BC, who waged war on Greece) protected the Jews who had stayed behind in Persia, rather than returning to Jerusalem with the first wave. It was the religious establishment of that first wave, led by Biblical figures such as Ezra, who anthologised and consolidated the foundations of what we now take as traditional Jewish belief and Biblical scripture dealing with the foundations of the world, the nation of

Israel and its rituals and early history.

The ironies of Persia's impact on early Christianity are in some ways even greater. They depend on the shadowy figure of Zoroaster (Zarathustra in the times of Nietzsche), who died about 551 BC. Like Buddha, no scripture was written down until hundreds of years after his death. Even so, the main body of his teachings predated Christianity, and they included: a universe of dualisms that contained good and evil, heaven and hell, light and darkness, and the personification of these dualisms in powerful spiritual beings (i.e. what we would know as a God and a Devil); a messiah, a saviour, born of a virgin; a final judgement and a resurrection.

The struggles of the early Christian church, with its rivalries and divergent bodies of teaching, included early strands of Gnosticism and, later, Manicheanism – derived at least in part from Zoroastrian thought; and the popularity of the Zoroastrian sect of Mithras, among Roman soldiers who had served on the front with Persia, included (although the historical record is disputed) the virgin birth on 25 December, and the sign of the cross in a circle. The debate is the extent to which all these elements impacted upon the final composite that Emperor Constantine in 325 CE officialised as the Christian faith in the key outlines we accept today.

The Persians, and Zoroastrianism, were extremely multicultural. Alexander the Great is said not to have died but to have seen the huge cultural and scientific merits of Persia and became a long-living king of Persia. The 'thought of Alexander' was in constant debate with the emergence of Islam, and this thought was regarded as important enough for the work of Aristotle and Plato to be curated and debated even while it was being lost in the European 'dark ages'. The 10th century Zoroastrian epic, the *Shahnameh*, the Book of the Kings, has one telling episode where the Roman Emperor (Vespasian) is brought before a Zoroastrian sage who lectures him on the teachings of each of the major world religions, including those from China and India, and concludes by chastising him in Christian terms, asking him what Jesus, the son of Mary, would think of Roman vanity and blood-lust. It is this kind of cosmopolitan cultural heritage, forced into a reductionist Shi'a fundamentalism by Western commentators on the 1979 Iranian Revolution, that confronted US and European negotiators over the issue of Iranian nuclear capacity. The Islamic conquest of Persia only achieved success towards the end of the 10th century and, until the 15th century, Persia was largely Sunni. One and a half millennia of deep culture preceded Islam, and impregnated Iranian selfhood as much as Islam. The work of great poets from the 13th and 14th centuries like Rumi and Hafez are cases in point. They praise God, but draw from mysticism and metaphysics.

But was even the Iran of the Ayatollahs dangerously fundamentalist?

The US antipathy towards latter-day Iran began with the supplanting of the US ally, the Shah Reza Pahlavi, in 1979. The US had invested much in his regime and, indeed, together with the British had engineered the demise of a government under him in what was recognised even at the time as a major petroleum scandal. But the revolution of 1979, together with its unpredictability, was characterised in US minds by the holding as hostage of US Embassy workers – followed by a failed US military rescue bid. The felt humiliation was immense. The US, funding the effort through the Saudis, greatly supported Saddam Hussein's effort to invade Iran in 1980.

For the Israelis, the concern about Iran's support for Hamas and Hezbollah, as noted in the last chapter, was a major reason for antipathy. The greatest element of fear directed towards Iran was, however, the deeply felt conviction that the Iranians were developing sufficient capacity to acquire nuclear weapons. With a secret but widely estimated 80 to 100 nuclear warheads of its own, Israel did not want to conduct a genuine balance of power with a nuclear-armed Iran. The balance of power with Egypt was US-managed, and in any case did not involve nuclear weapons. Having to enter a balance of power arrangement with Iran, predicated on nuclear mutual deterrence, would have involved Iranian leverage over a range of Israeli 'good behaviour', including possibly within Palestine. It would have meant an end to Israeli licence. Both US and Israeli public relations, therefore, worked assiduously to paint the Iranian regime as dark and as sinister as possible. The Iranians, for their part, hardly did themselves any favours with a cascade, several years long, of invective and religiously-inflected condemnation of the West.

As former UN Under Secretary-General, Giandomenico Picco, said however – he being the man who negotiated the end of the Iran-Iraq war, and the release of several Western hostages in Lebanon up to 1992 – there has never been a Shi'a or Iranian-masterminded atrocity against a major Western target. Moreover, Iran's support for Bashar Assad as President of Syria is not because of his own Shi'a affiliation. Assad's branch of Shi'a is Alawite, which has significant syncretic beliefs – such as a Trinity, being descended from the fallen angels and subject to repeated reincarnation (including as Christians) as they make progress towards heavenly reinstatement, observing Christmas and the feast day of Mary Magdalene, and a form of mass which uses wine – and is not recognised as Islamic at all by many Sunni scholars. To secure a more favourable attitude from Sunnis, and the majority Sunni population, the first President Assad, Bashar's father Hafez, took a pragmatic line and made the faith in Syria appear as Sunni as possible. However, he was himself the leader of the Ba'ath party, and this was dedicated to secular modernisation.

Although Ayatollah Khomeini did recognise the Alawites as Islamic, the alliance with Syria probably owes much more to securing allies in the region, i.e. it is as much to do with power politics as religion, as much to do with the long-term stability of a neighbouring state and its government, as being revolutionary. Given Alawite beliefs, Iran's support is certainly not fundamentalist.

It should also be pointed out that, although Iran supports Hezbollah and Hamas, it has encouraged and funded neither to do outrageous things against Israel. There has been no mass attack, no rolling waves of suicide bombs. There have been homemade rockets from Hamas, and a defence of Lebanon from Hezbollah. In short, the policy seems to have been one of violent harassment and damage, not of destruction.

The deep reason for Israeli antipathy towards Iran is to do with a balance of power fuelled by nuclear weapons. And this is exactly the reason for Saudi Arabia's antipathy towards Iran. Quite apart from the vaunted Sunni-Shi'a division, there is a simple question of power politics and regional hegemony.

Antipathy between Saudi Arabia and Iran

That the two states are Sunni and Shi'a is true, and this has a bearing on their often volatile relationship, but is not a sole determinant. Certainly Iran was furious that Saudi Arabia supported and funded Saddam Hussein's invasion of Iran, using among other things chemical weapons. However, during the Presidency of Mohammad Khatami, Iran made huge efforts to establish a *rapprochement* with the Saudi state and the two signed a security pact in 2001.

However, the US-led invasion of Iraq in 2003 was a huge turning point. Regime change led to the unintended, or under-estimated consequence of empowering the Shi'a majority in a country previously led by a Sunni despot. It meant an Iraqi tilt towards Iran and, instantly, the region's balance of power was destroyed. Thereafter, the Saudis saw Iranian plots everywhere – for instance, in the Arab Spring in Bahrain, where many protesters were Shi'a (in a Shi'a majority country), and which was suppressed with Saudi military help – but, before then, Saudi and US antipathy to the rhetoric of President Ahmedinejad saw the creation of a hostility which has lasted through the Arab Spring to this day.

The US-led 2013 agreement with Tehran to limit the Iranian nuclear programme, even under the moderate government of Hassan Rouhani, and even with moderates dominating the Iranian Parliament from early 2016, has not been enough to placate the Saudis. The two states back opposing sides in the Syrian war – and, in any case, Saudi Arabia never had its own nuclear weapons in the regional balance of power; it had a US nuclear umbrella instead so, in that sense, could be said to be way ahead of the Iranians in final-status muscle. There is something to be said, which has been almost fully under-estimated by commentators, and that is Tehran's relative modernisation of its social freedoms – despite a religious policing of sometimes hugely rigorous dimensions – and overall modernisation of society, a society not dependent on imported labour as in Saudi Arabia, and thus without those kinds of internal pressures that come from alien populations within. And Iranian women can drive cars. Simply put, despite the seeming monolithic nature of the House of Saud, Iran may simply be the more stable and progressive society – and comes with a far greater cultural heritage and historical glitter than the descendants of desert tribesmen and cattle raiders. The balance of power may not fully hide a balance of perceptions and self-perceptions. For the Israelis, however, the balance of power is huge and is militarily demarcated and measured.

Israel and the planning of attacks on Iran

There has been no war at any time directly between Israel and Iran, but the attitude and approach towards Iran by Israel suggests an existential threat to replace that which once emanated from its immediate neighbours; so that, in addition to the internal threat articulated so well by Uriel Abulof, is an external one chiefly articulated by the possibility of a nuclear-armed Iran. It is not an existential threat in the sense of the demise of a homeland for Jews. That is what a Palestinian majority within Israel would do. It is a threat to Israel's sense of hegemony in the region, and the freedom that comes from that to act as it sees fit and to project power unimpeded. Insofar as that has become part of an identity, not only the fighting Jew but the power-projecting Jewish state, what Israel does not want is a genuine balance of power with a nuclear Iran.

Iran's rhetoric in 2012 included statements about eradicating Israel, about an Iranian attack to 'wipe them off the world's geographic history'.[17] But this was in response to a series of similar verbal volleys from Israel from May 2006, firstly to do with destroying Iran's nuclear facilities, but also, in the words of Vice Premier Shimon Peres, that 'the president of Iran should remember that Iran can also be wiped off the map'.[18] It would seem that, from 2006 to 2012, Israel seriously contemplated, planned and at one stage was ready to launch

---

[17]   Brigadier General Hossein Salamni on 24 September 2012: www.ynetnews.com/articles/0,7340,L-4285130,00.html
[18]   As reported by *The Jerusalem Post*: www.jpost.com/Israel/Peres-Iran-can-also-be-wiped-off-the-map

a pre-emptive air strike against Iran's nuclear installations. It would seem that, at least in one such strike, the US air force would have been involved. In 2010, Israeli senior military personnel publicly questioned the wisdom of such strikes,[19] but in November 2012 Prime Minister Netanyahu reiterated the possibility of such a strike, even without US support.[20] As late as 2013, retiring defence minister Ehud Barak said that the Obama administration was preparing detailed plans for a strike.[21]

The strikes never came but, in 2013, a series of assassinations of Iranian nuclear scientists took place. Moreover, as far as we know from rumours and leaks, it would seem that all of the plans were predicated on the facilities being able to be hit – but the Iranians had dispersed them within mountainous terrain – and that an attack would not encounter disabling resistance, Israeli warplanes being far superior to Iranian ones and probably able also to elude Soviet-supplied anti-aircraft missile defences. No one seemed to contemplate a different form of Iranian response – sending up its air-force not to engage the Israelis, but to bomb Jerusalem and Tel Aviv.

A meditation

The diplomatic problems of the Middle East, especially those between Israel and its perceived enemies, are immense. The situation is made more complex in that Israel's external threats, requiring an appropriate 'securitisation move', are to an extent mirrored by internal threat, requiring a securitisation move that is not yet sensible. The need for an external threat is one that may have roots in a deep psychological need – always the readiness must be to react to a powerful force outside – derived from historical experience and reified discursively into an Iran of today with, simultaneously, all the attributes of modernity and a host of evil antiquities. Iran bears on its shoulders the Nazi appropriation of Nietzsche's Zarathustra, and not the cosmopolitan history and culture of incorporation, tolerance and multiculturalism.

The bomb becomes the clinching point. It was the Israeli point of decisiveness. No one else in the region had it. Therefore, an Israeli and Jewish hegemony could not be challenged. The prospect of challenge, but only insofar as there would be mutual deterrence and balance, was a request too far. Even though Henry Kissinger viewed his ideal world order as a

[19] www.timesofisrael.com/barak-netanyahu-wanted-to-strike-iran-in-2010-and-2011-but-colleagues-blocked-him/

[20] www.bbc.co.uk/news/world-middle-east-20220566

[21] www.haaretz.com/israel-news/ehud-barak-u-s-has-contingency-plan-for-surgical-strike-on-iran-1.496471

concert, or regional concerts, that produced equilibrium, the Israelis could find no equilibrium from a history where they suffered from radical disequilibrium. Iranian rhetoric certainly did not help, but nor did US perceptions of Iran which reinforced Israeli fears.

As a case example of use to the Copenhagen School, the situation may have no peers – but not only in Abulof's formulation. Here we have a parallel between the formulation of Abulof and the perceived threat of Iran. In the face of such perceptions of threat, in the face of securitisation moves, no amount of diplomacy or correct balances of foreign policy formulation – using any and all of Allison's models – may allow us, certainly for now, to find a way forward. And, as for the hapless Palestinians, with only the most rudimentary apparatus for diplomacy and foreign policy formulation – encamped upon and dependent on an enemy for fundamental basics like water – there is no discernible autonomous future.

8

The World Unites and Disunites: Someone Must Try to Keep It Together

As World War II slowly ground to a close, the allied powers began plotting a new global architecture. A series of key meetings was held. Some were summits involving only the most powerful allies, as at Yalta in 1945 – which brought together for the last time Roosevelt, Churchill and Stalin – and others involved all 44 allied states. Yalta stands out as the summit meeting that was entirely Realist and certainly cynical, as the Big Three divided Europe into zones of influence and occupation. All three leaders were comprehensively briefed, but to an extent the division was always going to be largely determined by control of the final battlefields. The race for Berlin and to occupy as much of Germany as possible resulted in what became known as West and East Germany until the fall of communism in 1989. However, the multilateralism of other meetings, although stamped by great power influence, did allow certain smaller power concerns to emerge. The foundation of what became the World Bank and IMF at the Bretton Woods Conference of 1944 could not avoid US economic power, without which there could have been no post-War multilateral financial order; but the 1945 San Francisco Conference to establish the United Nations had some interesting pushback from states that were not great powers – such as Australia.

The Australian ambassador at the San Francisco Conference, later a considerable academic writing on the character (and desirability) of a pluralist multilateral world, was John Burton. It was he who led the pushback against a Security Council originally proposed as having even greater powers than it now has. A Security Council was needed in the light of the often directionless League of Nations – a concert of great powers able to call the tune in times of crisis (assuming those great powers could agree on the tune), or at least a Council that reflected who had won the war, and who could determine among other things how not to lose what they had gained. Their interests would be inserted at the apex of the new organisation. Burton argued for a greater voice to be accorded to the General Assembly. The new world architecture could not be so predicated on hegemony that emerging states, destined to grow dramatically in number, would not wish to join it.

In some ways, however, what was outstanding about the new UN was not its political and diplomatic centre-piece but its specialised agencies. UNESCO was in some ways a sop to the intellectual classes that had provided a normative rationale for war against Fascism, and now they had a chance to urge the end to war altogether on the assumption that 'since wars begin in the minds of men', the cultivation of those minds would lessen war.[22] It neatly avoided the power politics and state interests that determined the rationale, nature and extent of war in terms of gains and losses. Agencies to do with world health, world development, the extension of concern for refugees and labour practices all suggested a world architecture that was concerned with functional cooperation. However, it was a functionalism directed for the most part towards the newly developing states and, insofar as it was organised technical and economic assistance from the top down, it was also in the first instance an expression of hegemony.

The debate over the Security Council, its true reflection of a world decided as much if not more at Yalta than San Francisco, the debate over the meaning of the functional agencies, all suggested that no one at the outset supposed that the new position of UN Secretary-General could become a decisive office in international relations.

The Secretary-General and the Arab-Israeli conflicts

The personality and drive of the Secretary-General, especially in the light of imprecise language defining the position, is critical. But such qualities only work if the incumbent has impeccable judgement and secures allies. We have noted how the Commonwealth Secretary-General, later a rival of Perez de Cuellar in the race for the UN post, Shridath Ramphal, was able to be highly instrumental in the case of Zimbabwean independence. But both the Commonwealth and the UN positions are calibrated as senior international civil servants, at high ambassadorial level; and, while certainly free to exercise 'good offices' in acts of persuasion and negotiation, the Secretary-General is not meant to exercise executive, i.e. self-conceived and self-directed functions. The position's role has evolved, depending on how new forms of 'good practice' have become accepted as 'normal', or how far the

---

[22]   Richard Hoggart, *An Idea and its Servants: UNESCO from within*, Piscataway NJ: Transaction, 2011.

great powers in the Security Council have consciously rolled them back. A constant tension has accompanied the relationship between UN Secretary-General and Security Council. In terms of extending new forms of 'good practice' until they become normal, the past-master has been Kofi Annan. He also was able to appoint his own Deputy Secretary-General and, in that way, build not only an internal support apparatus but, more importantly, the high Secretariat as a force in its own right, alongside the Security Council and General Assembly. However, the most activist and dynamic Secretary-General was Dag Hammarskjold – but he paid for this with his life.

Hammarskjold was the second of eight Secretaries-General up till 2016. It might be helpful to look at each of them against the backdrop of one of the most problematic parts of the world, the Middle East and particularly the Israeli state and its wars in the region.

Trygve Lie (Norway) was Secretary-General from 1946-52. His tenure coincided with the UN Mandate over Palestine which was meant to take over the Israeli independence process from the British Mandate. The UN officials complained that the British were far from cooperative and it is clear that, although UN figures worked very hard in a rapidly deteriorating situation, that what was already volatile would become dangerous and incendiary. Israel declared independence in 1948, and war with its Arab neighbours broke out. A comprehensive military victory was won by Israel, which in the process greatly enlarged its UN Mandate borders. The new borders were given the name, the 'green lines', meaning the lines of armistice agreed at the end of the war.

If Lie had been unable to prevent war, or the unilateral enlargement of Israel, Dag Harmmarskjold (Sweden, 1953-61) played a critical role in the diplomatic pressure against the 1956 Anglo-French-Israeli invasion of the Suez Canal. Granted he required strong US backing in the UN for his stand, but his definitive activism was clear. What he did not seek US backing for, or indeed any Security Council backing for, was the insertion of the first UN peacekeeping force in the Sinai, to stand between Egyptian and Israeli lines. He did this through the General Assembly – but no other Secretary-General has been able to bypass the Security Council on matters of peacekeeping. He himself received Security Council authorisation for the peacekeeping force sent to the Congo in 1960, as huge violence broke out on the independence of the former Belgian colony. But it was his work in the Congo, and the superpower conflict that was waged by proxy African parties and forces, that attracted fierce criticism. When his plane blew up over the northern Zambian city of Ndola, just south of the Congolese border, suspicions raged that it was an assassination – but no one has conclusively demonstrated whether it was the US or the Soviet Union that carried out the killing. The Zambians probably spoke for an emerging world that admired him. To this day, the shrine Zambia built to him, directly beneath where the plane exploded in the sky, is maintained – as is a mile of Swedish pines in every direction radiating outwards from the shrine.

His successor, U Thant (Burma, 1961-71), had a tenure that coincided with the 6 day 1967 war, in which Arab forces were again defeated, and the Egyptian military machine categorically demolished. There is much controversy over U Thant's role in the days building up to the war. Egypt's President Nasser had requested the withdrawal of the UN peacekeeping force in the Sinai. That, together with his massing of military might on his borders persuaded the Israelis that an Egyptian attack was imminent, and this led to the devastating Israeli pre-emptive strike. Whether U Thant could have negotiated more forcefully with Nasser, whether he misunderstood Nasser, whether he could have withdrawn the UN force very slowly, are all questions after the fact. The 1967 war saw Israel once again expand its borders, particularly in Syria; and it conquered Sinai up to the Suez Canal and the West Bank up to the Jordan River. The last year of U Thant's tenure also saw the fierce conflict between Jordanian and Palestinian forces – the so-called 'Black September' war, when the Palestinians felt betrayed by the Jordanians – and the PLO was forced out to new exile headquarters in Beirut. In his entire Secretary-Generalship, when huge stakes were involved in the Middle East, U Thant was able to accomplish no decisive intervention.

Turmoil in the region, but also diplomatic breakthroughs, coincided with the Secretary-Generalship of Kurt Waldhein (Austria, 1972-81). However, none of these primarily involved Waldheim. The surprise attack by Egypt to regain the Sinai in 1973 was followed by a series of intensive negotiations that featured, above all, Henry Kissinger. President Sadat's historic and surprise visit to Jerusalem in 1977, the Jimmy Carter convening of Sadat and Begin at Camp David in 1978, featured no central role for the UN Secretary-General. The Israeli invasion of Lebanon in 1978, the Iranian Revolution of 1979 and its diplomatic fallout with the US, and the US-supported Iraqi attack on Iran in 1980 all essentially bypassed the best efforts of the UN Secretary-General. It was not as if Waldheim was idle. He and his office were simply not central to these world events.

Perez de Cuellar (Peru, 1982-91) was Secretary-General during the second Israeli invasion of Lebanon (1982), the prelude to which saw a UN peacekeeping force repeatedly ignored and ineffectual as both Israeli and Palestinian forces transgressed what was meant to be a ceasefire. It was during his tenure that the first *intifada* broke out in 1987, and his term of office concluded as the first Gulf War erupted in 1991. The UN was involved as a site of intense diplomacy over this war, but the huge military coalition that retook Kuwait was led by the US. It was US diplomacy that persuaded even Syria to be part of the military effort to restore Kuwait as a Westphalian state.

Boutros Boutros Ghali (Egypt, 1992-6, apart from Trygve Lie and Dag Hammarskjold the only non two-term Secretary-General, largely because of his difficulties with the US) was in charge of the UN during the Oslo Accords of 1993 and 1995, but although the Accords were based on UN Security Council resolutions, Boutros Ghali was not a principal in those negotiations. Nor was Kofi Annan (Ghana, 1997-2006) a principal at the Clinton-brokered Camp David talks between Chairman Arafat and Prime Minister Barak, in an effort to salvage the Oslo Accords. The second *intifada* broke out in 2000 as a response to the failure of Camp David. Ban Ki Moon (Korea, 2006-16) coincided with the 2006 Lebanon war, and all three Gaza wars, 2008-9, 2012, 2014, without being able to influence the course of events in any of these.

The Security Council is the centre

None of this is necessarily to diminish the efforts of successive Secretaries-General – although some efforts and some Secretaries-General were better than others. But, despite the best efforts of probably the two greatest office-holders, Dag Hammarskjod and Kofi Annan, to enlarge the capacities and freedom of movement of their position, with a degree of success, neither could finally act as a free or executive agent, and both were beholden to the Security Council. The best a Secretary-General can hope for is to create and sustain an office that is, in some way – a nuanced way – able to help shape Security Council resolutions, and help drive their implementation.

Despite the apparent inabilities of the UN to solve all world problems, the Security Council has passed a huge number of resolutions addressing them. The Israeli-Palestine issue, and the principles that should shape any negotiated outcome – followed by the Oslo process – were prefigured in Resolution 242. However, having been passed in the Security Council with unanimity, it has hardly been the case that a Security Council member like the US has applied sustained or successful pressure on Israel to observe the principles of 242. So the derivative problem is not that the Security Council fails to act as a star-chamber multilateral body, but that bilateral diplomatic and political interests constrain or determine its members over and above multilateral agreements. Lip service is paid to the Resolution, without determination that it be the compulsory cornerstone of a Middle Eastern 'solution'.

The other problem of Security Council resolutions can lie in the wording. Resolution 1973 over Libya was just imprecise enough to permit NATO forces a free-rein in missile and aerial attacks on Gaddafi's regime. China and Russia, as members of the Security Council, were furious over the licence the US and its allies extracted from the resolution – but perhaps should also have recalled, disciplined and sacked their ambassadors to the UN who let such imprecision and its possibilities slip through.

If the five permanent members with their veto rights find it hard (a) to police the world in an agreed manner and (b) find it hard to police one another – as in the case of Libya – what is to be made of the pressing question of whether to enlarge the permanent membership of the Security Council. After all, a star-chamber of the five victors of World War II, even with China now properly represented, is hardly representative of the full power structure of the world, and certainly not of its emerging configurations of power. Should there be a seat for a Middle Eastern state? If that is Saudi Arabia, what does that mean for the Saudi 'double game' of being simultaneously Westphalian and supportive of Islamic insurgencies against Westphalian states? If it is Saudi Arabia, what does that mean in terms of the Sunni-Shi'a divide in its grossest terms? What does it mean in terms of Iranian participation in international affairs? Should Africa have a permanent member? Who should it be? Until recently, the economically most powerful state was South Africa. In one year, it has slipped behind Nigeria and Egypt. But this slippage is based on terms of calculation. Basically, change the equations and you change the result. But, with such available imprecision, how is a choice made? And, if the permanent membership is enlarged, do all the new permanent members have the veto? The 'club' would be unwieldy and prone to paralysis then. But can you have a star-chamber with some permanent members enjoying greater powers than other permanent members? The new UN Secretary-General will have to advance possible ways forward on this issue – to the Security Council in the first instance.

The specialist agencies and high commissioners

Some of the deepest value of the post-War UN is the work of its specialised agencies. The work of the World Health Organisation (WHO), the UN Children's Emergency Fund (UNICEF), the UN Development programme (UNDP), and the UN High Commissioner for Refugees accomplish huge good, and would have to be invented if they did not exist. If anything, these four agencies require considerable expansion and support.

More controversially, the work of the UN High Commissioner for Human Rights is valuable, not just as a defence of human rights *per se*, but because of the readiness of the High Commissioner even to criticise Security Council members. It is a key watchdog within the UN system of even the most powerful UN members. The High Commissioner's mandate derives from the General Assembly – and, if anything vindicates the stand taken by John Burton at the foundation San Francisco Conference of the UN, it is this.

The slow creep of 'normal' new powers

Dag Hammarskjold, under the so-called 'Peking Formula', a term derived from his work in securing the release of 17 US airmen held by China as a non-UN member, allowed the Secretary-General a free hand in the **implementation** of a peace and security mandate – although that mandate could not be created by himself for himself. Generally, it had to come from the Security Council. But this allowed an **operational** freedom, and creativity. In addition, Kofi Annan secured the right to appoint his own Deputy Secretary-General which, as noted above, allows the Secretary-General a degree of guaranteed support in his (or her) operational freedom and creativity. The Secretary-General is constrained by the demeanour of world politics, especially as it is developed by great power interests and veto rights. But sufficient room in which to manoeuvre becomes for the Secretary-General perhaps his (or her) greatest asset. The next Secretary-General, to be chosen in the second part of 2016, may come down to a nomination by the Security Council, for voting by the General Assembly, either of a candidate who is able and prepared to exercise creativity – or, as very often in the past – a candidate who can be trusted to make the right noises but not actually get in the way of the Security Council.

A meditation

It might be thought that the specialised agencies, like the predecessor organisations to the European Community and Union, concerned with functional and technical cooperation, could pave the way to closer political union in the United Nations. This cannot be the case. Firstly, the agencies are specialised outgrowths of a UN diplomatic and political arrangement which is circumscribed. Some room for manoeuvre might be carved out, perhaps a lot of room from time to time, but only within this circumscription. Secondly, the agencies did not come first – even though some are carry-overs from the time before World War II, but they were suborned to, firstly the League of Nations, and then given their role in post-War life very much as instruments of the UN. They cannot develop a later political union out of coal and steel, as in the case of Europe. They are co-terminal with the parent body and will live and die as it lives and dies, or be subsumed into yet another successor organisation. Thirdly, the functional cooperation largely concerns actions and programmes to help the deprived world, or the disaster-hit world. It is not as if UNICEF has huge programmes to help homeless children in the US or UK. However, the US and UK contribute much money to UNICEF to help others. In short, there is no functional cooperation as such between rich and poor states. The agencies exist in a hierarchical 'functionalism', just as the Security Council exists in a hierarchical relationship to the General Assembly.

Having said that, the popularisation of the UN is such – including a plenitude of honorary 'Goodwill Ambassadors' for specialist causes, e.g. Angelina Jolie, David Beckham, Shakira, Jet Li – means that the UN has entered a public consciousness that cannot easily be eradicated or its functions and causes minimised. If Angelina Jolie speaks for refugees, even the most hard-hearted government must at least appear to listen to her on her visits, and echo at least her sentiments even if they do not create the programmes of assistance she espouses. When Barcelona Football Club wears UNICEF as a label on the first team shirts, and every fan's facsimile shirt- whether legal or rip-off – carries the same UNICEF label, that specialised agency and its work will become an international element of general knowledge. A curious populist horizontality has come to accompany the political hierarchy of the UN. We thus enter a curious moment in the organisation's history. The new Secretary-General may have greater constituency in his or her support than those who went before.

9

The Excluded Fights Back: China's Economic Multilateral Diplomacy

China entered the world as a communist state in 1949, after a century of imperial occupation, Japanese conquest and colonisation, civil strife with warlords, and bloody struggle between the nationalist forces of Chiang Kai Shek and Mao's Red army. The China that was won by Mao was in ruins. Not only that, it was immediately ostracised by much of the world. The US recognised the rump nationalist regime that had fled to Taiwan as the government of China, and denied Beijing diplomatic recognition and a seat in the United Nations. This also meant exclusion from the UN Security Council, and therefore a place at the 'top table' of global diplomacy. Insofar as the Security Council comprised the victors of World War II it could be argued that Chiang's forces did more of the fighting against the Japanese than Mao's – and this was true. But it is not that the communist forces did not engage the Japanese at all. There were very bloody battles. However, as an expression of global power, the Security Council was incomplete without Beijing – although, here again, it could be said that the China that was won by Mao was hardly powerful in 1949. Even so, the issue became the first serious politicisation of the UN structure – where a government of a vast territory was denied a place because of the emergence of Cold War politics. The problem for China was that it was also excluded from a lot more.

The Chinese 'Three World' theory, discussed earlier in this book, was part of a political response in the mid-1970s to exclusion. It proposed the formation of China's own political alliances and blocs, in the face of exclusion or marginalisation from others. Even after the *rapprochement* with the US in 1971 and 1972, and the assumption of its UN Security Council seat, Chinese suspicions of the superpower world were high. However, it took the Chinese even longer to gain entry to the world's global economic institutions. The US, in particular, were reluctant to allow this. And, even with eventual entry, China's almost default foreign policy strategy kicked in with plans to form its own alternative global economic structures. It was prepared to do this at great cost – but it hoped for very great long-term returns, not only economically, but it terms of the political leverage that economic hegemony would bring.

Excluding architecture

The post-World War II architecture included institutions for cooperation (e.g. the UN), for close quarter collaboration (e.g. what became the EU), for what was called 'harmonisation' (e.g. the Organisations for Economic Co-operation and Development (OECD)). This was apart from the financial institutions (e.g. the World Bank and IMF) which were formed for highly constrained but effective forms of economic regulation to accompany the facilitation of capital flows. Here, the circulation of capital became more important than its mere accumulation. As long as it was a circulation dominated by the West, all was well with the World Bank and IMF. We shall return shortly to that. The practice of 'harmonisation' in the OECD was one where capitalist countries, by consultation and research, did not develop too far apart from one another, and each was able to remain fiscally in touch with the others at all times. In many ways it was the OECD that furnished the post-war triumph of global capitalism and prevented it from being a house that could have fallen apart.

Its political counterpart, comprising the most economically powerful countries, was the G7 – sort of like a political Security Council of the OECD. The developing world, in the form of the NAM, established its own counterpart to the G7, the G77, which campaigned for a more egalitarian global economic order. The entire late 1970s and early 1980s quest for what was called a 'New International Economic Order', aided and abetted by high-level expert groups such as the Brandt Commission,[23] was a key agenda item of the G77. China, however, was not included in the World Bank, the IMF, the OECD, or the G7 – and it was not even invited to join the G77, which was founded in 1964, until 1981. China might have wanted to lead the developing world, but was still to an extent distrusted by it.

The G77 was the developing world's response to the exclusive nature of the G6, as it first was, founded in 1975. The G6 included France, Germany, Italy, Japan, the US and the UK. It became the G7 with the addition of Canada in 1976. These were the world's richest capitalist economies and were part of the Cold War architecture which seemed dated when the Cold War died down after the fall of Communism in 1989. Even so, it took until 1997 before Russia

---

[23] Independent Commission for International Development Issues, *North-South: A Programme for Survival*, London: Macmillan, 1980.

was added to the group and it became known as the G8 – although the G7 has met without Russia since its annexation of Crimea in 2014. This expressed the continuing use of the group as a political as opposed to a purely economic device. No invitation has ever been extended to China.

It was only in 1999, with the establishment of the G20, that China secured a seat at an expanded top table. The G20 included Argentina, Australia, Brazil, Canada, China, France, Germany, India, Indonesia, Italy, Japan, Mexico, Russia, Saudi Arabia, South Africa, South Korea, Turkey, the UK, the US and the European Union. Its establishment recognised that global capital and its artefacts – production and trade – were no longer at the command of only the great post-war powers. The G20 disposed of 85% of the world's gross product, 80% of world trade, and contained two thirds of the world's population. But this means that, as late as 1999, the exclusionary practices of world politics had kept China from full membership of the global economic system's summitry. The UN's Security Council was well and good, but China's economic outreach needed the friends and partners it found within the G20.

China's inclusion in the world's financial and economic organs has been uniformly slow. The World Trade Organisation (WTO) was established in 1995, but China only gained membership in 2001. The World Bank Group was established in 1944, but China gained membership only in 1980. However, the real issue at stake with Chinese membership of the World Bank is voting strength. It was only in 2010 that China's vote rose from 2.77% to 4.42% - based on capital made available to the group. The strongest vote in the World Bank is that of the USA with 15.85%. Japan's is second with 6.84% and this leaves China in third place, ahead of all European powers, Russia, India and Saudi Arabia. But the gap between 15.85% and 4.42% is a huge one, leaving the US as still the dominant player in the World Bank, and reluctant to allow the Chinese any further increase in capital subscription and voting strength. The US Congress has also been reluctant to ratify the 2010 agreement on expansion of Chinese strength in the IMF. Even former Federal Reserve Chairman, Ben Bernanke, on 2 June 2015, blamed Congress for the Chinese banking initiatives discussed in the next section of this paper.[24]

But 2009 also saw agreement that the G20 would replace the G8 as the main economic summit of the world's wealthiest nations. In a sense, the limit to Chinese strength in the World Bank only added to the determination of China to use the G20 as a springboard and kind of unifying device for its own plans towards global economic strength.

---

[24] http://www.cnbc.com/2015/06/03/us-congress-pushed-china-towards-aiib-bernanke.html

It is in this light that we can see the rise of Chinese interest in the foundation of other banks, and of a sort of 'Security Council' within the G20 – one that this time, in a reversal of its own Cold War exclusion, excludes the Western powers. By that I mean the BRICS consortium is well placed to assume a commanding role in the G20. All the policies and strategies involved will likely come together in a visible global vision at the 2016 G20 in the beautiful lake city of Hangzhou, China.

It will have taken eight years for China to be given a turn to host the G20. Since 2008, the annual event (although there were two G20 summits in both 2009 and 2010), has been hosted in Washington DC, London, Pittsburgh, Toronto, Seoul, Cannes, Los Cabos (Mexico), St. Petersburg, and Brisbane; and was hosted in Antalya (Turkey) in 2015.

Of banks, roads, belts, and great corridors

There is an emerging alternative, perhaps rival, global architecture. This will reprise and expand greatly all that China has practised for many years, and that is transport corridors of rail and road, but now also lined with infrastructure for community benefit. It will involve new multilateral banks in key regions, but they will be banks in which voting is not based on strength of capital subscription, but purely on a one-member-one-vote basis, without any Chinese veto – even if China is the main financier. It will see an overarching role for the new BRICS Bank, and it is this that is likely to make its first major programme of loans at or near the time of the G20. It will also see, in addition to transport corridors across land, maritime corridors and, here, there will likely be a role for a refurbished Chinese navy. With this, the global economic geography would also assume a geopolitics that will see the return, minus Russia at this stage, of global superpower rivalry – albeit couched in the friendliest of language and the most careful of diplomacy.

The first key area of direct rivalry is in the Asia-Pacific, with the US launching the Trans-Pacific Partnership (TPP) – albeit with some domestic misgivings in member countries about job security in a liberalised trade zone. China is not included in the TPP, but has secured agreement in 2014 from regional countries for an Asia-Pacific Free Trade Area – an ambitious and upscaled outgrowth of earlier Doha Round talks. This will require some years of planning and strategic preparation – but the immediate challenge to the TPP will be the new Asian Infrastructure Investment Bank (AIIB), which, although not concerned directly with trade, will hugely influence capital flows in the region. Figures vary, but it is to be capitalised at least at $50 billion, with China providing half if not more of this figure. Australia, with US prompting, at first said it would not join the AIIB, but then changed its mind. A non Asia-

Pacific power, the UK, also wishes to be associated with the new bank. Western powers perceive the effect the AIIB will have in economic development and fiscal flows in the region. We shall dwell upon the implications of the name of the bank – especially what is meant by 'infrastructure' - below. For now, if the AIIB is a challenger to US plans in the region, then China is also launching a challenge to Russian interests in the area of the Silk Road.

This is where the intriguing vocabulary of 'one belt one road' arises – for the land route will also be an infrastructural corridor, with communications and energy systems and facilities as part of a provision which will go far beyond transport. The road will be paralleled by a maritime 'Silk Road' route, so that China's links with the countries to its west and south-west will be comprehensive ones that will also considerably develop those countries themselves. This 'one belt one road' project is being capitalised at some $50 billion, about half if not more coming from China.

An extension of the Silk Road project will be the 3000 km southern route through Pakistan. It will link China to the Indian Ocean by a direct transport artery. It will also have an electronic communications and energy infrastructure and, more importantly to Pakistan, it will open up for the first time the capacity of Pakistani governmentality of its problematic northern territories. At a stroke, these territories, home to Taliban and other bandit societies, will be made accessible, and the populations of those territories will be able to enjoy developmental benefits and thereby be weaned from the outlaw organisation of their lives. This is expected to involve some $46 billion of Chinese investment and, of course, has raised great interest in India, Pakistan's rival regional power, with Prime Minister Modi himself now interested in a new relationship with China.[25]

Everywhere one looks, the Chinese are making plans and achieving agreements with powerful and strategic partners. $50 billion is proposed for new infrastructure, transport and steel projects in Brazil.[26] There is talk of a trans-Amazon transport link across Brazil and Peru, to be built by the Chinese.[27] And, of course, there is Africa – where much talk and speculation is concentrated on the size and nature of Chinese investment. Some of this suggests Chinese investment of as much as $100 billion by as early as 2020. By the same year, according to the Chinese Premier, Africa-China trade will double.[28] This is a rather huge projection, and it remains to be seen how it will

[25]   http://www.bbc.co.uk/news/world-asia-china-32718384
[26]   http://www.bbc.co.uk/news/business-32747454
[27]   http://www.bbc.co.uk/news/world-latin-america-32858944
[28]   http://www.scmp.com/news/china/article/1505388/trade-africa-will-double-2020-li-

be done. If there is not greater African productivity of goods or materials sought by China, then will it be in goods from China to Africa – in which case, where is the African absorptive capacity? Chinese ambitions towards Africa may not yet be fully blueprinted, but the signals are certainly being given that huge investments are being contemplated. Much of this, as in the Silk Road, Pakistan, and Brazil, will be infrastructural. The final completion of a Cape-to-Cairo transport link, first proposed at the dawn of colonialism by Cecil Rhodes, may be ironically due to China – itself being imperialised by the West at the same time Africa was. Transport is of course a hallmark of Chinese involvement in Africa. The Tazara Railway, linking Zambia to the sea via Tanzania, at the time of white stranglehold on transport routes south through Rhodesia, controlled by white rebels, and South Africa, controlled by Apartheid, remains the template for all visions of what the Chinese can do for the continent. The more recent huge plans to build a transport corridor across southern Democratic Republic of Congo, with infrastructural provision, and which aroused great antipathy from the West, is an updated version of the same template.[29] That too, as in Pakistan, would have increased governmentability and enhanced development in a volatile and troubled region. But, if 2020 is a target year, then the G20 in 2016 may represent a best-possible moment for the specifications of what investments will entail.

A meditation

How does foreign policy conceive of cultural animations? It seems a distant question to associate with Chinese global economic outreach. However, earlier in this chapter I used the term 'default strategy'. If excluded from global organisation, then the post-War Chinese history has been to seek, with immense patience, the moment of inclusion – but, simultaneously, seek not just inclusivity but centrality within alternative forms of organisation. These alternatives are conceived and constructed, again with immense patience and the patina of partnership with selected others, with extremely grand capacities. They become not only alternatives but challenges to those structures and organisations from which China was once excluded. The grand – almost grandiose – alternatives/challenges have China as a central planner and player. They situate China in the centre of the world. Perhaps the West left it far too long to begin the process of bringing China in from the cold, in from the Cold War – and then made the mistaken assumption that, once finally in, the Chinese would become an important, but also just another large player in the global diplomatic and economic architecture. Once 'in', there could be placed upon China an entire range of control variables, not least from the voting power of the US in the IMF, and repertoire responses and

---

keqiang-tells-ethiopia-conference
[29]   Chan (2013), pp 31-33.

protocols of operation of other institutions. Certainly China, in its new institutions, may be intent upon new repertoire responses – perhaps genuinely sympathetic ones to the needs of non-Western development in emerging nations. There may be a genuine outreach here, but also perhaps a modernised and globalised form of chauvinism. Also, perhaps certainly in terms of irony, the exclusion and marginalisation of the 'Middle Kingdom', the 'Central Kingdom', may now rebound upon those who were the excluders – as China seeks to be, this time in genuinely global terms, the kingdom that is the centre of the world.

*The central argument of this chapter draws from: Stephen Chan, *A Prognosis and Diagnosis for China and the 2016 G20: The Politics of a New Global Economic Geography* (Brighton: Institute of Development Studies, 2016).

10

The Separability of Jihad

The rituals of slaughter

There is a scene in the Zimbabwean novel, *The Stone Virgins*, by the late Yvonne Vera which is so elegant it is only some pages later and after some reflection that the reader realises a ritual execution has taken place. The scene describes a beautiful tango. Anyone who has learned to tango will recognise the steps. Almost hear the music. The male partner makes a movement with his hand, upwards and curved as he spins his partner. As they come out of the spin he steps to the side like a matador with his hand stretching out and slightly rising in a flourish. In fact, there is a movement like this in every style of Tai Chi. People studying the ancient Chinese art for the sake of health will not appreciate the martial intent. A blade has cut a throat, and the next movement is to step aside to let the body fall.

How it is done was best depicted by Eva Green in the otherwise terrible film, *300 Rise of an Empire* where, as a warrior Persian Princess, she decapitated Spartan warriors smoothly with a knife. You can see they die with the first incision. The removal of the head is almost gratuitous. Those who have never been or worked in an abattoir, and who receive their meat cellophane wrapped clean and innocuous at the supermarket, will not know that the butchers seize each sheep as it comes forward from a chute. It is done by hand. One arm seizes the neck of the sheep, almost cradles it, and the other applies Yvonne Vera's tango slice. Both arms then seize the sheep and hang it on a meat hook, its head dangling from the cut, as the carcass is sent out in the most macabre exhibition of Fordism for the next butcher to begin the skinning and then others the dismemberment. The wrapping and packaging are done by machine.

This is basically the method of *halal*. A singular incision must cut through jugular vein, carotid and windpipe. In fact, despite controversy, it is largely merciful. The animal dies or at least loses consciousness as the incision reaches the carotid. The only real difference between that and the most traditional slaughter method of *kosher* is that the Jewish version requires both sides of the neck – jugular, carotid on both sides and windpipe in the centre – to be severed in a single stroke. The objective in both is the draining of blood. When ISIS executes its victims in the propaganda videos, this is how it is done. Every Western special forces soldier recognises it. They've been taught to do it too.

The rituals of cleansing

The Biblical book of Leviticus, meant to have been written shortly after the exodus from Egypt in 1290 BCE, was probably compiled by the priests of Ezra after the return from Babylon in 539 BCE. This meant the rituals of cleansing, purportedly designed to preserve hygiene under primitive conditions, had lasted as cultural practice for a considerable time. The rituals are extensive and pervasive. There is much washing of hands. The rituals are also gendered in that women at the time of menstruation and shortly afterwards are required to undertake especial cleansing and bathing. Menstruation was a sign of both womanhood and the female condition, which was one of uncleanliness.

Such rituals pervade Middle Eastern practice. The Zoroastrian practices of ancient Persia require many such rituals, and a huge number of these have found their way into the 19th century religion of Bahai, viewed as heretical in modern Iran, as recorded in the prophet Baha-u-llah's short scripture, the *Kitab-i-Aqdas*, where page after page is devoted to hand and other washing.

The problem here is that slaughter of animals and the draining of blood by cutting through the throat's systems was also meant to promote cleanliness and hygiene. Blood is a contaminant if exposed to the air and left to attract microbial infestation. In that regard it is like urine. The problem is that, in the slaughter of prisoners and hostages by ISIS, the method of slaughter is in fact associated with cleansing. At the very least, it is a problem of irony.

A gross genealogy of jihad

I use the term, 'gross', as debate on jihad among Islamic scholars can be dense. There is in general an antipathy against a vulgar use of the term to denote war and rebellion – even though rebellion as a cause of war can be complex. War and violence in any case are a 'lesser' jihad. The 'major' jihad is to do with struggle, especially spiritual struggle. To take a Christian analogy, Jerome's struggle in the wilderness as he set about translating the scriptures into Latin would have been jihad. However, I use the term here in its contemporary and common manifestation to denote rebellion that turns to international war. Note that, typically, rebellion is described as having just cause. This is the subject of debate. What seems unjust are the deliberate indiscriminations in the conduct of war – targeting mass non-combatants – that both Augustinian precepts and the Geneva Conventions prohibit.

Again, having said that, mass slaughter – evoking casual but powerful uses of the term 'genocide' – is a terrible commonplace in today's world. There have been an estimated 2 million fatalities in the vast killing fields of Democratic Republic of Congo in the last 20 years, and an incalculable amount of gendercide – all of this sparked off by the genocide in Rwanda in 1994, as that conflict and its atrocities spilled into neighbouring territories. My students who were hardened Zambian peacekeeping soldiers in Rwanda sent me anguished letters as to what they found, and the unending numbers they had to bury. I have had personally to count bodies at mass execution sites in African wars and, in the end, simply filed reports of my estimates as, after several hundred, I no longer felt like counting.

I do not want to fall into Mary Kaldor's trap to do with 'new wars' and their lack of rationalities.[30] Those rationalities are there, even if they seem terrible and terrifying. But I do concede that what makes jihad seem terrifying is the very deliberate presence of rationality, ideology, doctrine and faith – often presented with great learning. It is this marker, 'atrocity with calculation and faith', that is attached to jihad; and it is a movement on from the Nazi exterminations of Jews in World War II which were 'atrocity with calculation and ideology'. The presence of faith generates a global controversy, rather than a proper global debate precisely because faith is connoted with atrocity.

Having said that, I wish now to give a brief disquisition of three 'insurgent', 'fundamentalist' groups that have become somewhat indistinguishable in our vocabulary. Each has become almost a trope for something awful and threatening. Each, however, is quite different from the others – and certainly in the case of the first: to atrocity, calculation and faith we might add some romance (if, for a Western readership, it is not *haram* to do so). The three groups are the Afghani Taliban, Al Qaeda, and ISIS.

The original Taleban

The movement began as a response to Western policy that left Afghanistan in the hands of rapacious warlords – who had been financed and armed, through Pakistan, and with Saudi funds (some US$40 billion) at the

---

[30]   Mary Kaldor, *New and Old Wars: Organised Violence in a Global Era*, Cambridge: Polity, 2012.

instigation of the US, to defeat the Soviet occupation. When the Soviets withdrew, the warlords predated on their own people, but the West had achieved its objectives and retained no interest in a beautiful country that no one had successfully governed as a single sovereign entity for any length of modern time.

The following story is dismissed by some as Taliban propaganda. Ahmed Rashid, the celebrated Pakistani journalist, considers it authentic. Even if not true, its use as a legend, as an illustrative and explanatory narrative, filled a need for a justifying foundation. That it should be filled in such a romantic fashion is what is of interest here.

Mullah Omar was a village priest in the Kandahar area. He was blinded in one eye as a result of fighting the Soviets. One day, the distressed parents of two teenage daughters sought him out. The local warlord had kidnapped the daughters and intended to use them as his concubines at his heavily fortified base. The parents had nobody left to whom they could turn. Omar should have been able to do nothing. But he was outraged and wanted to try. He rounded up a handful of Talibs (theology students). Together they secured one gun for every two of them. Then they assaulted the barracks of the warlord. Miraculously, they won. They rescued the girls and hung the warlord from the barrel of one of his own tanks. The legend was born and young fighters, sick of the despoliation of their country by the warlords, flocked to the banner of Omar and the Taliban was born. In itself, this should have been nothing more than a Robin Hood story – but the romance was allied to faith, and to an army of the faithful, a new nationalism, cleansed, seemed possible. A Taliban army, by now attacking with Toyota pickups mounted with machine guns, assaulted Kabul in 1996.

The warlord who held Kabul was Ahmad Shah Massoud. Like the Taliban, he was a Sunni Moslem, but a northerner and not from the Pashtun areas of the south. An ethnic dimension now opened up. Massoud was much admired in the West, not least as a hero figure by the likes of Bernard Henri Levy, the dandy intellectual gadfly with huge influence in Paris, who sought to ingratiate Massoud with President Mitterand. Massoud did have filmstar looks, and he wore Gucci boots under his traditional clothes. However, under the glamour, he did seem to have a genuine respect for human rights and, in particular, the rights of women. But he could not stand before the Taliban assault and withdrew north to his ethnic base. Osama Bin Laden, who had returned to Afghanistan shortly before the Kabul attack, having first gone there in 1979 to fight the Soviets, and who had enjoyed many adventures in Sudan and elsewhere since, ensured Massoud was assassinated the day before 9/11. Osama knew the US would come for him and he wanted the one formidable local enemy to be taken out of the equation. As it was, when the US and NATO forces did come, they used Massoud's Northern Alliance army as its spearhead, the NATO forces themselves being equipped with an entire two Pashtun interpreters. But most of the northerners didn't speak Pashtun either, and were hated by the south. Afghanistan was always going to sink into a civil war in which the Taliban had huge southern support.

Al Qaeda

The story of Osama Bin Laden always had an element of rich-boy-playing-warrior. However, he did commit most of his Saudi fortune to his causes. In his Afghan sojourn, he did finance much development. And he did become a good fighter. He was wounded fighting the Soviets. In his propaganda videos he has clear command of his AK47. Before his return to Afghanistan in 1996 he had declared war on the USA, both because of its presence in the 'holy places', i.e. on Saudi soil for Gulf War I, and his view of US attacks on other parts of the world. It is still a matter of controversy who first initiated Al Qaeda and exactly when, but Osama certainly had become its leader by 1996. Translated as the 'base' or 'foundation', Al Qaeda was meant to be not an Afghan organisation, but a foundation for global jihad. Luring the US into Afghanistan was meant to be the first major step of this jihad, both dispiriting US policy-makers and the public who would find themselves in a quagmire, and hoping the US would commit atrocities for global broadcast to a huge prospective jihadi audience. In short, the US would provide foundations for a global rebellion based on just cause.

Within a conscious step-by-step strategy, two things were noticeable. The first was that Al Qaeda did not conceive of its self-organisation as monolithic. There was to be no organogram with central command. It was deliberately designed as a cell organisation and members would be franchisees of an ideology, a faith, and an operational doctrine against a shared enemy. There would be no Caliphate until it was evident the US had been defeated or so thoroughly demoralised it withdrew from world hegemony, and especially its powerful outreach into the Middle East.

ISIS

The so-called Islamic State of Iraq and Syria (or ISIL, the L standing for the Levant, the countries of the eastern coastline of the Mediterranean) began life as a wing of Al Qaeda in Iraq. When it sought to muscle its way into Syria, during the meltdown occasioned by the failure of the Arab Spring and the chaos of repression and uprising, other Al Qaeda groups protested that their turf was being trespassed. Despite warnings from senior Al Qaeda leaders –

but by this time Osama had been killed and the franchise nature of the group militated against fully accepted central leaders – the Iraqis continued, recruited some 80% of the fighters from the Al Nusra Front (the Syrian Al Qaeda franchise), and declared itself as having both a new name and a central leader. He called himself Caliph Baghdadi, his name indicating he had come from Baghdad, where he had also taken a PhD. The idea of the Caliphate, an Islamic form of theocratic state, was a direct challenge to the prevailing Westphalian state system. Unlike Al Qaeda, who had intended to fight the West to a standstill before declaring a Caliphate – a state model for the rest of the Islamic world – Baghdadi began with the Caliphate and declared that the traditional form of Islamic state organisation would lead the defeat of infidel states. It wasn't just that his enemies were infidels. They were states in the current state system. Baghdadi's was a major statement in international relations.

The ideology in common

ISIS therefore seeks to fight Jihad for a new international state system. In a way this is more important than the one-dimensional accounts of its ideological origin, alongside the Taliban, Al Qaeda, and Saudi Arabia, in Wahhabism. Its political ambitions differ from those of the Taliban and Al Qaeda; and Saudi Arabia seeks to be a Westphalian state while placating as far as it can powerful Wahhabist pressures within. Until March 2015, there was in the Western press a *single* article of more than 3000 words on the beliefs and motivations of ISIS. This was in the *Atlantic* magazine[31] – so, to a huge extent, the West was fighting something about which it had no articulated knowledge. There has been a plethora of books since, including some by authors with Arabic language and experience. The core of almost all these works is precisely the tensions within Saudi Arabia – simultaneously a US ally, a source of much oil used in the West, a counter-balance after the failure of Iraq to the emerging strength of Iran, and the source – through non-state means - of much of the early finance for Al Qaeda and ISIS. It is an imposing contradiction, in the face of which the US has no known policy.

In 1744, two men led an army out of the desert and briefly seized much of what is now Saudi Arabia. The two who formed an alliance were the tribal leader, Muhammad Ibn Saud, and the preacher, Muhammad Ibn Abd-al-Wahhab. Although the fortunes of the Saudis waxed and waned before the 20th century, and the House of Saud betrayed the Wahhabists in the struggles for the country, they were never to shake the Spartan desert ideology out of their society. In 1979, undisputed rulers of the country which was now recognised as a Westphalian state, and rich beyond their wildest dreams

---

[31]   Graeme Wood, 'What ISIS Really Wants', *Atlantic*, March 2015.

because of oil revenues and the huge inflow of petrodollars after the 1973 oil price rises, the House of Saud was radically shaken by a Wahhabist uprising against their opulence and the presence of foreigners, meaning US oil companies, on holy soil. A group of insurgents seized the holy mosque in Mecca and, clearly with much financial support and military training, held out against sustained Saudi assaults for three weeks. All of Mecca had to be evacuated. It was a terrible embarrassment that the House of Saud could not protect the holiest of places. In the end, it was precisely foreigners who overcame the resistance of the insurgents – although accounts differ as to whether they were French special forces who had officially converted to Islam for the occasion, Pakistani forces, or even CIA personnel. The captured insurgents were executed in public, but it is thought that – shaken by the event – the House of Saud found it necessary to craft a special deal with the religious establishment of the country.

In short, the deal was that in return for continued rule, and for continued US presence in an otherwise holy land, that land would be made more holy by an effective clerical control over education, juridical matters, social matters including questions of gender equality, and including questions of social discipline. Furthermore, a blind eye would be turned to non-state Saudi support for ideologically like-minded groups elsewhere, even when they were battling the US.

The educational control is to an extent evident in the ease of adaptation of Saudi schoolbooks on religious studies by ISIS in the captured city of Mosul. Juridical matters pertain to the use of Sharia jurisprudential principles and precepts. Social conservatism speaks to not only a lack of civil liberties and rights to political organisation of critical organisations, but to the restrictions on women. This includes the infamous prohibition on women driving cars. Social discipline along lines of older corporeal practice – although it should be said it is also not dissimilar to 17th century European practice – include punishments to do with lashings and beheadings for what would be non-capital offences elsewhere in today's world.

The Saudi religious education texts took a line against infidels, and so were particularly attractive to ISIS (although these may have been hurriedly revised after their adoption by ISIS). In short, the controversial, provocative but key question is not how 'medieval' ISIS might be, but how like modern Saudi Arabia it might be or aspire to be.

Much is said about the austere nature of Wahhabism – although the continued opulence of the House of Saud must continue to test patience in the stricter realms of the clergy. That same clergy, however, benefits from wealth and ploughs it back into a huge raft of international endowments, scholarships, symposia and sponsorships. It projects a nuanced conservatism in a soft power that is entirely recognisable along the now classic lines of soft power enunciated by Nye. But there are two other key aspects of the doctrine, much harder and not 'soft' at all. One is that the world is due for a cleansing. At some stage, the true Mahdi, a cleansing figure, will appear to prepare the world for God's day of judgement. The doctrine has this clear eschatology. The second is that, in preparation for the Mahdi, just war or jihad should be waged against apostasy. This is broadly defined. It includes non-Sunni Islam, including Shi'a. And here is the essential point of just conduct in war or jihad: precisely because of apostasy, those so designated do not enjoy the benefit of just conduct towards them in times of war. They may be dealt with atrociously. The Mahdi will appear in the wake of the new Caliphate.

The exceptional Middle East

The end of the 20th century and beginning of the 21st saw the erosion of the huge strides towards secularism undertaken in the Middle East: Nasser's Egypt from the revolution of the Free Officers of 1956; the controversial triumph of the Ba'ath party, with Hafez Assad seizing power in Syria in 1970 and Saddam Hussein in Iraq in 1979 – all following behind the revolution of Ataturk in Turkey in 1922. In all those areas, forms of Islam are rolling back the era of secularism; and the revolution in Iran in 1979 saw the end to the Shah's rule and, with it, the installation of the reign of the Ayatollahs. The Shi'a in Iran bear some special comment. This comment is not an exoneration of the clerical regime. It does indicate however a degree of pragmatism and, above all, of centralised theocratic direction which is effective as well as pragmatic; some would say also more sophisticated than its Wahhabist antagonists.

The key differences between Sunni, with its Wahhabist faction, and Shi'a lie in issues to do with succession from the Prophet (each therefore claims the authentic line); and with the issue of the Mahdi. In Sunni Islam, the Mahdi is yet to come. In Shi'a Islam, he has come but was then hidden (in 'occultation') and will come again. There are also differences in terms of interpretation both of the Sharia, and the sayings of the wise men of Islam. The Sunni Wahhabists believe the Shi'a are apostate; in addition there are regional cultural issues which are magnified and distorted to prejudices, so that many Saudi Sunni believe that the Shi'a do not wash properly and spit into their food.

The Shi'a, with its majority population in Iran, and as noted in an earlier chapter, look beyond Islam in the sense that they are mindful of a very long uninterrupted legacy from the days of empire rivalling and confronting that of the Romans, of curating and developing Aristotelian and Platonic thought when it was all but lost in the West, and – strange as it may sound – of the multicultural nature of the Persian empire and the cosmopolitan knowledge of different faiths evident in Zoroastrianism, with its influences on Christianity, well before Islam. It is more accommodating of Sufism, which is also considered apostate by the Wahhabists. A different cultural impulse accompanies Shi'a to that of the Sunni faith and there is none of the desert-born Spartan minimalism and austerity of outlook associated with the teachings of Wahhab.

Modern pragmatism derives also from the work of the French-trained sociologist and philosopher, Ali Shari'ati, who had a major intellectual influence on the revolution in 1979. He had progressive views on women and, in particular, recognised the agency of women when it came to fighting for a cause, especially a nationalist or liberationist cause. There is a curious echo of this in the Hamas constitution, where there is explicit provision for women to decide of their own volition to fight for the nationalist Palestinian cause, without permission being required from any man, husband or father.

There is also, again as noted earlier, the testimony of former UN Under Secretary General, Giandomenico Picco, who negotiated the end of the Iran/Iraq war – the Iraqis under Saddam Hussein being spurred on and financed, through Saudi Arabia, by the US – and then the release of Western hostages in Lebanon in 1992. As Picco said, there has not been since that time a single Shi'a-led or inspired major atrocity against any Western target. The Western argument with Iran, he implies, is a political one, albeit given confessional dress. But the revolution ended Kissinger's aspiration for developing the US alliance with the Shah; there was US embarrassment over the taking of embassy hostages in the early days of the revolution in 1979; there was the need to side with Saudi Arabia in terms of the perceived Shi'a threat to Sunni interests and, in any case, to ensure a balance of power between Saudi Arabia and Iran; more recently, with perceived Iranian steps towards nuclear capacity, to ensure a balance of power that was carefully controlled between Iran and nuclear-capable Israel.

Many of the above comments need nuancing and reference to other examples. Saddam may have been secular, and he may have included women in his Cabinets and advanced significantly female education, but he also oppressed minorities, the Kurds in particular, and his atrocities were also directed against Kurdish women. Those same Kurdish women, who are largely Sunni, today form effective fighting units against Sunni Wahhabi ISIS. Isis is certainly not above the murder and mutilation and denigration of

Kurdish female fighters and Kurdish women in general; and the ISIS treatment of Yazidi women constitutes genuine mass atrocity. Yazidis are not Islamic, although they have certain Sufi leanings and rituals. They are not Christian either, but exhibit a centuries-old syncretic blend of beliefs. They are very easily regarded as apostate by ISIS.

A meditation

The curious reward for Wahhabi martyrs seems drawn from a boy's own spa. Dark eyed virgins will attend every need, including curiously carnal needs in a heavenly setting. By contrast, the propaganda videos for female Kurdish fighters very consciously aim for support from the West and Western women. It is a 'we too wish to be free like you, because we *are* like you' message – except of course they live in a country which will never be free as an independent state, and their Western audiences will for the most part never imagine they need a state which can guarantee them the constitutional right to be free women and equal persons. The binary of fighting woman and black-clad ISIS Islamic assassin is instant, without the need for political interrogation.

The need precisely for such interrogation is so that our treatment of Islam, its sub-divisions, its proposed just causes, and its contentious problematics, is not devolved only to an imaginary – devolved precisely to that realm used so well by recruiters for ISIS, in which everything is flat-packed and assembled according to instructions to form a perfect rubric of justice, justification, simplified politics and apostasy.

Having said that, it is also precisely the fleshly aspects of the ISIS phenomenon that bear at least some passing comment, but which should not substitute for political interrogation that is also informed by religious appreciations and methodology. The need to kill by ritual is common to a battlefield in Syria and a public square in Saudi Arabia – but so too in the public squares of China. The difference is one of the intimacy of execution. The executioner in Saudi Arabia swings a sword. It should be swung as a back stroke, i.e. like a backhand in tennis, so that the jugular and carotid are cut first – but the executioner need never touch his victim. The ISIS method aims for precisely the same target, but as in Yvonne Vera's tango, must almost caress the victim's head and neck to accomplish the execution. Each death becomes an expiation which echoes just cause in its work of cleansing. It is a moment for us of horror. For the executioner, it is a moment of atrocious holiness. In the intimacy with another's death we have a question not only of politics but of the psychology of jihad. It may be a lesser jihad, but its depths are as great as those of the major jihad. It may be in the social origins of that psychology, rather than in foreign policy, that we might best begin some meaningful work on jihad.

11

The End Days of the World System? Before Armageddon the Long Nights of Ignorance

The Copenhagen School of International Relations stressed the discursive foundation of how we approach the world. How we think of the international, what we admire and particularly what we fear, creates a structural formation to which policy-makers respond, or which they try to manipulate. They cannot instantly recreate it as something new and different. By the end of a long process of responses it might be different – but it won't be unrecognisable from the original public discourse. Insofar as policy makers seek to create threats of a 'previously unknown' international relations, and then seek public discursive support, they first seek recourse to a battery of media and personalities of validation – the use (or misuse, a misuse to which the academics concerned are amenable, and culpable,) of the 'New Mandarins' in Chomsky's term, of 'expert' validators for newly created policies that require such public discursive support is now part of the lexicon of policy-makers.[32] The creation of Iraq as a possessor of 'weapons of mass destruction', imminently launch-able at the West, might as well have used an advertising agency for the catch-phrase, almost the jingle, 'weapons of mass destruction' – but a host of sudden Middle Eastern experts lined up behind the subterfuge, especially those who instantly conflated Iraq with Islamic threat, with Axis of Evil; and led the public to believe it was a do-or-die 'clash of civilisations'.

The discourse became one of fear. Part of this was clearly understandable after the attack of 9/11, but the linking of this fear to Iraq was the deliberate manufacture of a misunderstanding. Discourses of fear and misunderstanding depend, in the first instance, on simplifications. The creation of simplification as discourse is a curious work of art – but, as the

---

[32]   Noam Chomsky, *American Power and the New Mandarins*, NY: Pantheon, 1969.

public responds within this discourse, and piles discursive pressure on policy-makers to act, those same policy-makers are able to apply stock and repertoire responses. The response has to be by repertoire as there is neither time nor organisational inclination to create something new. If all defence mechanisms have, at huge cost, been geared to certain sorts of war, it has to be that sort of war if instant action is required. An entire military machine cannot be re-calibrated and re-equipped; and even parts of it would require doctrinal re-orientation. Thus, after 9/11, it was not enough of a response to hunt down terrorists in shadowy enclaves. The policy and military machines needed to hit another state – an enemy within a clearly identified state – one susceptible to planning mechanisms long developed and rehearsed for invading another state. Clearly, the enemy lived in that state. After the identification and invasion of Afghanistan came the identification and invasion of Iraq – the latter unleashing the very same Islamic enemy that had been created for discursive purposes and then developed a discursive life of its own, participating in a virtuous (or vexatious) circle that linked public and political discourse most intimately.

The threat moves indoors

The slow realisation that 'Islamic terrorism' doesn't require a central host state – and the even slower realisation that Osama Bin Laden deliberately lured Western forces into an Afghan conflict so that it could be a site of 'war for public relations' in order to condemn the 'Western Crusaders' in the creation of an Islamic discourse – was painful as well as slow, as it required exactly a recalibration of repertoire. And, if the enemy no longer had a location that could be attacked; indeed, if often the enemy was within our own states; then discourse led on from fear and simplification to a species of police-state panics – none of which came close to defeating the 'enemy' and, indeed, probably elevated its recruitment figures. Suddenly, there were even more enemies.

The new mood of internal securitisation did not necessarily lead to any sophistication in thought, as domestic policy – surveillance, policing – utilised repertoire responses in exactly the same way foreign policy had. However, gradually the realisation dawned that Al Qaeda was different to the Taliban in Afghanistan; that Osama, while sympathising with the Taliban, probably used them as much as helped them, in order to launch his global war using the cellular structure of Al Qaeda. It was a Hydra-headed monster: cut off one head and another dozen grew from the bloody neck. Osama didn't mind losing Afghanistan as his operations spread far beyond their early epi-centre. And he won time – as Western forces encamped themselves in Afghanistan and then, in a gesture almost calculated to help Al Qaeda's discourse, waded into Iraq. Al Qaeda had no previous presence in Iraq and it was able to launch-pad its Middle Eastern operations from there courtesy of the US-led intervention.

But, because Al Qaeda was cellular, and its repertoire could morph from country to country, and in the end Osama became only one of several regional leaders, intelligence never had a central focus – a coordinating point in which all knowledge could make sense, or at least achieve coherence. And then when, slowly, it did begin making some forms of linked but disparate sense, the intelligence community was most reluctant to take the advent of ISIS seriously. The community had just worked out some repertoire for dealing with Al Qaeda. Did it have to start again? Surely it could analyse ISIS in the same way as it had learned to analyse Al Qaeda. And, besides, there was almost no knowledge of ISIS before its sudden advent. Critically, this applied even to the academic world. No expert mandarins could explain the phenomenon, let alone explain it in a way that made sense in policy and public discourses and the desirable linkage and intimacy of the two discourses. Those discourses at least had to retain their public air of simplicities and fear.

As for Osama, had he somehow managed to retain leadership of the amorphous organisation, then killing him was probably the worst thing the US could have done. Now, there certainly is no central leadership, and the many heads of the Hydra are multiplying. Sometimes, in their quest to multiply, remain viable, or simply survive, they have even fought ISIS. We might perhaps have needed Osama as the new dragon lurched into view.

Out of a blue sky

The term, 'out of a blue sky' was used by Western commentators, stunned that the Soviets could launch a full-scale invasion of Afghanistan in 1979 without any prior indication that they were planning such a large operation. The failure of Western intelligence was that it was not looking at the Soviet Union with Afghanistan in mind. It was not so much 'out of a blue sky' as the wrong weather forecast. Similarly, consumed finally with the threat of Al Qaeda – and not just the Taliban which, by this stage, was a most convenient distraction almost planned to keep the West focussed on one place and not too many others – ISIS appeared 'out of a blue sky' and, before a blink of an eye, had conquered huge swathes of Iraq and Syria. The very expensively US-equipped Iraqi army melted like snow on a sudden hot day of a dramatically early summer. By this stage, Iraq and Afghanistan were receiving the greatest amounts of US military aid, outstripping the chief benefactors of old, Israel and Egypt – but to no avail. Apart from surprise, ISIS battle strategy was simply too much for an appallingly Generaled Iraqi army. And ISIS filled the voids created in the disorder of the Syrian civil war, and took over most of the Al Nusra organisation that had hitherto been fighting as an affiliate of Al Qaeda. But the coordination of the sudden move, its superbly equipped and mobile battle plans and doctrine, its huge fleets of Toyota pickups – all in the same colour, all mounted by Browning machine guns, all needing to have those machine guns bolted to a reinforced tray or bolted to the chassis of the Toyota, each one in exactly the same way and to the same battle-ready standard - spoke of an external provider not only of finance but strategy, doctrine and early training. Fingers pointed at the Saudis – but Western intelligence had nothing public to say about that, and the policy and public discourse was carefully maintained to depict Saudi Arabia as an essential, valuable, indeed noble ally. The social policies of the kingdom – public beheadings, lashings, the denigration and restraint of women – might have seemed the stuff immediately associated with ISIS in its conquered territories, but the fiction that was now discourse said in public that the two were not related.

The *Atlantic* magazine article of March 2015 posited that ISIS had an agenda, i.e. was not mindless; had highly sophisticated technological and media outreach, i.e. was not simple; had international reach in fact, i.e. was not a desert insurrection, and had a Wahhabi animation, i.e. espoused a body of thought. All these conclusions, within a brief and hurriedly argued article, seemed startling – and could only seem startling because the information it contained also came 'out of a blue sky'. The simplification of threat into something simply evil had not allowed for even a summary sophistication of evil.

Wahhab and the desert blues

The scholarship that has emerged, quite suddenly, on Wahhabism is often hurried and fails to make distinctions. In fact, Lawrence of Arabia first noted the joyless aspect of Wahhabi strictures as he visited one of his favourite oasis towns to find that coffee, singing, and flirting with women were suddenly *haram* or prohibited. It is exactly the joyless strictures which have characterised the sudden scholarship. Its austerity and puritanism make it an exact caricature fit for what a 'fundamentalist Islam' is meant to be. It also allows it to be automatically conflated, in a reductionist manner, without regional cultural differences and hugely different political agendas taken into account, with the Taliban and its social atrocities. All evil becomes the same, and it becomes generalised to the point of being amorphous. This can only get in the way of detailed analysis. It becomes a stereotype without anything complicating the brief that is sent up to political masters who seek only confirmation that a simple-minded one-dimensional Devil is stalking the world.

The teachings of Wahhab were in fact simple. Among Islamic scholars he is not regarded as a peer. He attained prominence and power as an ally of the early House of Saud, so that at a very early stage his work was used for politicised purpose. Betrayal by the House of Saud, realignment with the House of Saud, secret agreements with the House of Saud after the 1979 Siege of Mecca all continued and developed the politicisation of the desert teachings. In modern times, they have their politicised roots in the Sykes Picot agreement of 1916, which divided the Middle East into zones of possession and zones of influence between the British and the French. The feelings, inclinations, and preferred borders of the Arab peoples were as naught. The protestations of Lawrence of Arabia were as naught. But, insofar as a new Islamic State seeks to overturn the imperial borders and reunite the Arab Sunni peoples, and cleanse from Arabia apostates such as the Shi'a and Yazidis – never mind the Western imperialists of today – theirs is an anti-colonial and political agenda as well as any religious one. None of this might have come to pass if Saudi Arabia, as it was at time of independence in 1932, had remained poor. Oil was not discovered till 1938. Before then, it was one of the poorest countries on earth, reliant on tax charges levied against pilgrims to Mecca and Medina. The Spartan conditions of life then would have pleased Wahhab – but sudden wealth, greatly exacerbated after the price rises of 1973, brought political influence and a form of global political power, and modern Wahhabism should be seen in that light – as a key benefactor-in-tow. It is not something that can be analysed only in terms of its foundational roots.

It should be seen certainly in terms of its religious roots and teachings, but also in its political context, and its ideological impulses. Even the religious teachings have a modern dimension as they seek to impose themselves upon modern conditions and their social policies, the needs of modern public administration, and the speed of modern media and communications. ISIS has put into place a public administration for its conquered territories, it must deal with modern economics as it finances its huge operations and pays its armies of foreign fighters, and it deals with a massive communications and social media outreach capacity which it has fully mastered. It has to turn all of these things in the direction not only of religion but ideology. It is against the West. It is antipathetical to the West and anti-social to it, and recruits among those in the West who are anti-social. Those who attacked Paris and Brussels were criminals, recruited not to turn them into devout and learned Muslims, but into ideologised fighters who, already hardened, would welcome a justification – a form of just cause – in fighting against a system that had marginalised them and ostracised them.

It is not against the West only in terms of Western lifestyle. That lifestyle has echoes even in a socially-policed Saudi Arabia. It is against a Western state system in which Westphalia houses a hegemony of Western powers. It is against that hegemony. Its fight for an Islamic state system is to reverse international hegemony. If it is successful, Islamic State may prove to be no more radical in terms of its everyday workings than Saudi Arabia now is. But, until then, it is against Western outreach, certainly in the holy places, and certainly in terms of the direct expression of US hegemony in its support – physically in the Middle East – of Israel. It is not just Israel as Israel, but Israel as a bastion of Western hegemony. As for the more purely religious teachings of this form of Islam, there must be sounded notes of caution.

The impossibility of hermeneutics in foreign policy formulation

The problem with interrogating a body of religious teaching   is that the tools for interrogation need to be appropriate. Even with theological tools, there is no sustainable assumption that one theological system fits all theologies. Moreover, before the theology must come the text itself, and it must be appreciated in terms of the nuances of the language used and its cultural and historical context. Then there must be a certain hermeneutic sensitivity – an almost intuitive sensitivity, a spirituality if you like, that allows a penetration of the 'mysteries' of the text. The following checklist of what are essentially cautions applies to any effort to 'crack' a religious persuasion.[33] It is not possible to 'get to the bottom' of Wahhabism as a research agenda for combatting it. Such a teleological ambition distorts and pre-ordains the theological enquiry.

1. Before seeking authorities as interpreters of meaning, it is first necessary to read the foundation texts.

2. It is necessary to acknowledge and appreciate historical and cultural contexts.

3. It is necessary to acknowledge and seek to appreciate linguistic conventions and, in particular, the role and deployment of metaphorical reasoning.

4. It is necessary to acknowledge traditions of intertextuality, that is, a sacred

---

[33]   Drawn from my fuller checklist: Stephen Chan, 'Trauma and Dislocation in the Postsecular World: Religious Fervour and the Problem of Methodology', in Luca Maveli and Fabio Petito (eds.), *Towards a Postsecular International Politics: New Forms of Community, Identity, and Power*, NY: Palgrave Macmillan, 2014.

text is interpreted by a legal text, as in Islam; a sacred text is interpreted by a mystical text, as in Judaism; both texts are interpreted by an ideological text, as in religious Zionism.

5. Hermeneutics have a function of investigating both deep within as well as a scripture's effort at transcending itself, that is, its meaning is both deep and rises above itself.

6. There are centuries of epistemological and ontological debate, all of which form genealogies that backdrop and inform current debate.

7. Current debate can deliberately or by force of circumstance pervert and distort first principles of sacred teaching.

It is almost impossible to turn proper religious enquiry into a foreign policy brief or accord it much utilitarian use in foreign policy formulation. It allows no options for actions – precisely because religious interpretation generally reveals in the first instance options for understanding. Which option for understanding should be chosen for which option for action becomes, finally, guesswork. New policy repertoires can hardly be informed by guesswork – except that, at the moment, exactly such repertoires are being created by guesswork of the most superficial sort – and often they are bargained into place to satisfy competing organisational demands, and not to address seriously and deeply the issue at hand. This is true within a single government, e.g. that of the US, and is even more so of a multilateral organisation like NATO.

As for the rational actor who might, like a presidential messiah, make sense of it all, and call all the right shots from all the right decisions based on all the right judgements... well, the advent of President Trump hardly satisfies the hopes in that kind of vision of a rational actor who faces up to ISIS. For now, Trumpian or Trump-less, we face a protracted period of cycles and circles of simple policies and simple discourses. And with or without the defeat of ISIS on the plains of Nineveh, its vision of a different state order with a different normative inspiration has impacted hard upon the world.

12

A Meditative Coda: Diplomacy and the End of Foreign Policy as We Know It

The 'rational actor' figure, if conceived as a 'High Noon' type of Western sheriff, single-handedly facing down the gunslingers, does not have to be the President or Prime Minister. Chester Crocker, as US Assistant Secretary of State, essentially adopted the 'High Noon' image for himself in his tense, difficult, high-wire, high-stakes, protracted, but successful negotiations over the futures of Angola and Namibia and, as it turned out, impacting upon the prospective Apartheid-free South Africa.[34] He had, however, originally been an architect of Ronald Reagan's 'constructive engagement' with South Africa – whereby close relations were maintained with the Apartheid state, both for Cold War purposes and for access to minerals and the safety of Western shipping around the Cape of Good Hope; while largely gentle, if persistent, pressure was applied on the South Africans, not so much to reform their policies, but to apply those policies more gently. The Crocker of 'constructive engagement' was a man of the policy machine, an exponent of repertoire responses that were refined and fine-tuned; the Crocker of 'High Noon' became extraordinary because of extraordinary circumstances – unpredicted by US foreign policy outlooks. The Cuban army and Soviet pilots had defeated the South African Defence Forces at the battle of Cuito Cuanavale in Southern Angola in 1988. Without that, talks would have been impossible – let alone talks with much momentous consequences. Even so, Crocker was able to exhibit a licence unthinkable within his earlier incarnation as the cultured but still 'machine' policy-maker.

Perhaps John Kerry was able to bring some such licence to his negotiations with Iran over nuclear issues. He had, however, the support of President

---

[34] Chester A. Crocker, *High Noon in Southern Africa: Making Peace in a Rough Neighbourhood*, NY: Norton, 1993.

Obama, who clearly wanted a *rapprochement* with Iran – dealing with ISIS, melt-down in Syria and Iraq, working out how to deal with the Saudi double-game, working out how to deal with Israeli Prime Minister Netanyahu, how to deal with a re-emerging police state in Egypt, were all quite enough without having to posture hostilities with Iran as well. Besides, albeit in reductionist terms, a Shi'a balance to the feuding and volatile Sunni states might be enough of a wake-up call to get them to get their Sunni act together. The Kerry talks finally made progress, however, after the US – albeit with some Iranian prompting as to what approach they would respond to – decided to alter its demeanour; and began according the Iranian delegations the sort of inflected respect and dignity accorded not so much to an Islamic 'civilisation', but a 'great' civilisation with the sort of classical antiquity alluded to earlier in this book. But it had taken some time for this message to filter up the organisational processes, and through the repertoire analyses, of the State Department. And Kerry's change of tone was not made the subject of a media circus, as there was a public discourse of malign Iranian evil which had to be 'managed', having first been hysterically created in the days of Jimmy Carter, and sustained and developed assiduously since.

However, it is rare that a sole actor can emerge with such licence or nuance at the end of a machine process and discursive environment. Henry Kissinger sought to be the arch-duke of such licence, and to create both a dazzling refurbishment of the Westphalian state order and a testament to his own intellectual perceptions as a student as to what such a world order should be: hegemonic, but balanced; stable with equilibrium; pluralistic but led by a concert; a concert playing a predictable score, with room for solos, but with the US as its principal conductor. Often he dazzled merely to effect – or affect. But there is no one else like him, together with his perfidities and sacrifices of others, in post-War history. Many would still regard him as a war criminal, but his diplomatic skills are a matter of record.

But is his Westphalian state system safe? And, if it is not as safe as it should be, can foreign policy formulation and diplomatic capacity – even with occasional flourishes of creative licence – safeguard it?

Equilibrium and the balancing act of hegemony

Kissinger's era was one where a balance of power existed between the US and the Soviet Union. The Soviets bought into this kind of world system when they had acquired nuclear arms – it was the arms, and the power and leverage they projected, that were weighed in the balance. Everything else – numbers of allies, spheres of influence - was important but secondary to the fact that Mutually Assured Destruction (MAD) had been created as the anchor to the balance of power. It didn't matter that the US had more nuclear weapons, or better delivery mechanisms. Both sides could destroy the other – several times over – and so crude arithmetic was not decisive. The US might, therefore, have had greater arithmetic hegemony, but this did not disturb the essential equilibrium.

The Soviets were prepared to test the balance, tilt its scales a little, and did so with the Cuban missile crisis – but pulled back at the key moment of danger. But it showed that even hegemony could be contested within the equilibrium – sliding scales of capacity for destruction were permitted, so long as capacity for destruction was unimpaired, and no actual destruction occurred. Moreover, the world was divided into blocs, Western and Eastern blocs being spheres of hegemony; and, within each bloc, there was enough to be getting on with in terms of local balances and contestations.

The complicating factor in all this was China. Nuclear-armed and in a Cold War with both the US and the Soviet Union, it had the capacity to be a rogue actor within the balances of equilibrium. One of Kissinger's great triumphs was taking China out of the equation with his historic *rapprochement.* In a real sense, Kissinger calculated that China could be 'civilised', could be 'domesticated' within the system, i.e. learn to behave as a force that would not seek to tilt the scales – while enjoying such power and leverage as it had, provided the global equilibrium was not disturbed. It allowed the US and the Soviet Union to play a two-actor game, and made their 'rational calculations' of each other's behaviour easier.

However, it is good to remember what a radical step Kissinger took. The pre-*rapprochement* rhetoric of China could be shrill, and certainly sound dangerous. The labelling of the West as 'paper tigers' and its allies as 'running dogs' may have been drawn from classical Chinese theatre and satire, but to those without that cultural knowledge it sounded like impudence – only it was an impudence with nuclear weapons; it had fought a war against the US in Korea, and was supporting war against the US in Vietnam.

The seriousness with which such rhetoric was taken meant that, during the McCarthy anti-communist witch-hunts of the 1950s, the US State Department was purged of its Sinologists, its China experts like John Service having their careers abused and truncated. Looking back, it was not unlike the Islamophobia that is rising today.

A twenty first century equilibrium

But, as with China in the 1970s, a latter day equilibrium might require the bringing of new states, and new forces, into the world system – even if the world system has to change somewhat to accommodate them. The problem is that actors bring into the system instruments of contestation. The question is whether it is better to have those within the system – rebalancing the equilibrium perhaps; making it far more complicated than a two-actor game, certainly – than outside the system and ready to threaten the system. At least, at this moment of writing, insurgent groups that nevertheless want to be forms of a state do not have nuclear weapons. They may have 'fifth columns' within Western societies – but they at least are more amenable to social practices than nuclear weapons that were never controlled by any citizen bodies.

The future global environment, and its foreign policies, might depend less on the attractions of defining and definable 'rational actors', and more on finding ways forward in processes and organisations that will become much messier than before. There may have to be a greater marriage between foreign and domestic policies. There will be an end to stock repertoires and, hopefully, a (painfully slow) ending to simplicities and reductionisms.

The only rational actor worth having?

Graham Allison never meant his 'rational actor' model to refer to an individual leader, or a contained institution which was led or at least involved a leadership. It is public discourse which has romanticised the notion that an individual diplomatic superhero is possible. That was part of the discourse created around Henry Kissinger. It is the public perception of John Kennedy during the Cuban missile crisis – the angst-ridden president at the top of the perch, the buck having stopped at his feet, pondering huge existential choices – literally holding the power of destruction in his hands. It was never like that. It can never be so. It cannot be even with the reasonable start made by new UN Secretary-General, Antonio Guterres. He is, as described above, constrained like his predecessors. At the level just underneath, some possibilities once existed.

For, if the world of diplomacy needs a heroic figure, an archetype, so it is not simply a game of bargains and balances, and options within those bargains and balances, then there is still the very real legend of the UN official, Giandomenico Picco. Whereas Chester Crocker called his memoirs, *High Noon in Southern Africa*, after the Gary Cooper western of the lone sheriff, Picco called his *Man Without A Gun*.[35] In order to secure the release of Western hostages in the Lebanon crisis in the 1980s, he let himself be kidnapped time and again, so that he would be dragged blindfolded and

---

[35]   Giandomenico Picco, *Man Without a Gun: One Diplomat's Secret Struggle to Free the Hostages, Fight Terrorism, and End a War*, London: Crown, 1999.

bound to the chiefs of the terrorist networks, so he could negotiate at the 'highest terrorist level' and did something in diplomacy which is rare – which no diplomacy or diplomat undertakes today and, with huge risks, might be what the becalmed and tense and violent world needs – a leap beyond repertoires; a leap into darkness.

Bibliography

Uriel Abulof, 'Deep Securitization and Israel's Demographic Demon', *International Political Sociology*, 8:4, 2014.

Adekeye Adebajo, *The Curse of Berlin: Africa after the Cold War*, London: Hurst, 2010.

Sydney D. Bailey, *Four Arab-Israeli Wars and the Peace Process*, Houndmills: Macmillan, 1990.

Mary Boyce, *Zoroastrians: Their Religious Beliefs and Practices*, Abingdon: Routledge, 2000.

Jonathan A.C. Brown, *Misquoting Muhammad: The Challenge and Choices of Interpreting the Prophet's Legacy*, London: One World, 2015.

Stephen Chan, *The Commonwealth in World Politics: A Study of International Action 1965 to 1985*, London: Lester Crook, 1988.

Stephen Chan, *Out of Evil: New International Politics and Old Doctrines of War*, Ann Arbor: University of Michigan Press, 2005.

Stephen Chan, *Southern Africa: Old Treacheries and New Deceits*, New Haven: Yale University Press, 2011.

Stephen Chan, *The Morality of China in Africa: The Middle Kingdom and the Dark Continent*, London: Zed, 2013.

Shahram Chubin and Charles Tripp, *Iran-Saudi Arabia Relations and Regional Order*, Oxford: Oxford University Press, 2005.

Natana J. DeLong-Bas, *Wahhabi Islam: From Revival and Reform to Global Jihad*, NY: Oxford University Press, 2008.

Steve Itugbu, *Foreign Policy and Leadership in Nigeria: Obasanjo and the Challenge of African Diplomacy*, London: I.B. Tauris, 2016.

Henry Kissinger, *On China*, London: Penguin, 2012.

Paul Moorcraft, *The Jihadist Threat: The Re-Conquest of the West?*, Annapolis: Naval Institute Press, 2016.

Dan Plesch and T.G. Weiss (eds.), *Wartime Origins and the Future United Nations*, Abingdon: Routledge, 2015.

Ahmed Rashid, *Taliban: Islam, Oil and the New Great Game in Central Asia*, London: I.B.Tauris, 2001.

Geoffrey R. Watson, *The Oslo Accords: International Law and the Israeli-Palestinian Agreements*, Oxford: Oxford University Press, 2000.

T.G. Weiss, *What's Wrong with the United Nations and How to Fix It*, Cambridge: Polity, 2012.

T.G. Weiss and Rorden Wilkinson (eds.), *International Organization and Global Governance*, Abingdon: Routledge, 2014.

Note on Indexing

E-IR's publications do not feature indexes due to the prohibitive costs of assembling them.

If you are reading this book in paperback and want to find a particular word or phrase you can do so by downloading a free PDF version of this book from the E-IR website.

View the e-book in any standard PDF reader such as Adobe Acrobat Reader (pc) or Preview (mac) and enter your search terms in the search box. You can then navigate through the search results and find what you are looking for. In practice, this method can prove much more targeted and effective than consulting an index.

If you are using apps (or devices) such as iBooks or Kindle to read our e-books, you should also find word search functionality in those.

You can find all of our e-books at: http://www.e-ir.info/publications

www.ingramcontent.com/pod-product-compliance
Lightning Source LLC
Chambersburg PA
CBHW050743030426
42336CB00012B/1639